ADULT MATH FOR BEGINNERS

The Ultimate Step by Step Guide and A Comprehensive Adult Math Refresher

By

Reza Nazari

About Effortless Math Education Inc.

Effortless Math Education operates the www.effortlessmath.com website, which prepares and publishes Test prep and Mathematics learning resources. Effortless Math authors' team strives to prepare and publish the best quality Mathematics learning resources to make learning Math easier for all. We Help Students Learn to Love Mathematics.

All inquiries should be addressed to:
info@effortlessMath.com
www.EffortlessMath.com

ISBN: 978-1-63719-547-5

Published by: **Effortless Math Education Inc.**

for Online Math Practice Visit www.EffortlessMath.com

Introduction

Welcome to *Adults Math for Beginners*. For many of us, our mathematical journey was a path taken years, perhaps even decades ago. Over time, the formulas, equations, and principles we once knew have faded, replaced by new knowledge and life experiences. Yet, there are moments in our adult lives when the need for math resurfaces, be it for a new job, helping children with homework, or just for personal growth.

This book is designed to reintroduce you to the world of mathematics in a way that feels approachable and relevant. We understand that diving back into math can seem intimidating, especially if it's been a while since you last studied the subject. But fear not, for this guide was crafted with the adult learner in mind.

Adults Math for Beginners strips away the complex jargon and focuses on the core principles, presenting them in a manner that's both engaging and relatable. We highlight real-world applications, ensuring that you can see the practical use of each concept you relearn. Our aim is not just to reacquaint you with math but to make it a useful and valued tool in your everyday life.

Whether you're embarking on this journey out of necessity, curiosity, or a desire for personal growth, we're here to guide and support you every step of the way. Let's rediscover the world of mathematics together, and prove that it's never too late to learn.

How to Use This Book Effectively

Congratulations on taking the proactive step towards enhancing your math prowess with **Adults Math for Beginners**. This book is tailored to help adults, like you, to reacquaint themselves with essential mathematical concepts in a manner that's both intuitive and applicable.

Whether you're preparing for an exam, assisting someone else in their studies, or simply broadening your intellectual horizons, using this guide effectively will be paramount to your success. Here are some tried and tested strategies to ensure you make the most of this resource:

✓ **Lay a Strong Foundation:** Before diving into advanced topics, ensure you have a solid grasp of the basics. Each chapter of this book has been designed to build upon the previous one. It's essential to thoroughly understand each concept before proceeding to the next.

✓ **Consistent Study Sessions:** Procrastination is the enemy of progress. Instead of waiting until the last minute, set aside 20 to 30 minutes daily for focused study. This approach, often termed "spaced repetition," has been proven to reinforce learning more effectively than cramming.

✓ **Active Learning:** Don't just passively read the content. Engage with it. Attempt the exercises, solve problems, and ensure you understand the rationale behind each solution. If you stumble upon a challenging problem, mark it and revisit it later.

✓ **Review Regularly:** At the start of each study session, take a few minutes to recap what you learned during your previous session. This repetition will help cement your understanding and recall of concepts.

✓ **Test Yourself:** At the end of each chapter, you'll find a set of practice questions. Treat these as mini-quizzes, testing your comprehension of the chapter's content. If you find particular areas of weakness, revisit those sections of the chapter for clarity.

✓ **Simulate Real Exam Conditions:** Once you feel confident in your understanding, attempt the comprehensive practice tests located at the end of the book. Do so under exam-like conditions: find a quiet space, time yourself, and resist the urge to peek at the solutions.

✓ **Assess and Adjust:** After completing a practice test, review your answers critically. Analyze both your correct and incorrect answers to understand your thought process. This reflective practice will help you identify areas for improvement.

✓ **Stay Curious:** Remember, the joy of learning math doesn't just lie in getting the right answers, but in the journey of problem-solving itself. Stay curious, stay engaged, and enjoy the process of rediscovery.

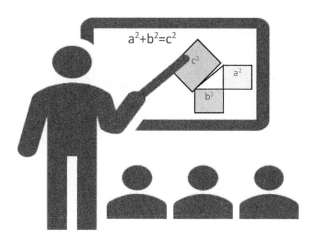

Looking for more?

Visit <u>EffortlessMath.com/Adults</u> to find hundreds of Math worksheets, video tutorials, practice tests, and much more.

No Registration Required.

Contents

1 Fractions and Mixed Numbers

Math topics that you'll learn in this chapter:

- ☑ Simplifying Fractions
- ☑ Adding and Subtracting Fractions
- ☑ Multiplying and Dividing Fractions
- ☑ Adding Mixed Numbers
- ☑ Subtracting Mixed Numbers
- ☑ Multiplying Mixed Numbers
- ☑ Dividing Mixed Numbers

1

Simplifying Fractions

- A fraction contains two numbers separated by a bar between them. The bottom number, called the denominator, is the total number of equally divided portions in one whole. The top number, called the numerator, is how many portions you have. And the bar represents the operation of division.

- Simplifying a fraction means reducing it to the lowest terms. To simplify a fraction, evenly divide both the top and bottom of the fraction by $2, 3, 5, 7,$ etc.

- Continue until you can't go any further.

Examples:

Example 1. Simplify $\frac{18}{30}$

Solution: To simplify $\frac{18}{30}$, find a number that both 18 and 30 are divisible by. Both are divisible by 6. Then: $\frac{18}{30} = \frac{18 \div 6}{30 \div 6} = \frac{3}{5}$

Example 2. Simplify $\frac{32}{80}$

Solution: To simplify $\frac{32}{80}$, find a number that both 32 and 80 are divisible by. Both are divisible by 8 and 16. Then: $\frac{32}{80} = \frac{32 \div 8}{80 \div 8} = \frac{4}{10}$, 4 and 10 are divisible by 2, then: $\frac{4}{10} = \frac{2}{5}$ or $\frac{32}{80} = \frac{32 \div 16}{80 \div 16} = \frac{2}{5}$

Example 3. Simplify $\frac{40}{120}$

Solution: To simplify $\frac{40}{120}$, find a number that both 40 and 120 are divisible by. Both are divisible by 40, then: $\frac{40}{120} = \frac{40 \div 40}{120 \div 40} = \frac{1}{3}$

Adding and Subtracting Fractions

- For "like" fractions (fractions with the same denominator), add or subtract the numerators (top numbers) and write the answer over the common denominator (bottom numbers).

- Adding and Subtracting fractions with the same denominator:

$$\frac{a}{b} + \frac{c}{b} = \frac{a+c}{b} \qquad \frac{a}{b} - \frac{c}{b} = \frac{a-c}{b}$$

- Find equivalent fractions with the same denominator before you can add or subtract fractions with different denominators.

- Adding and Subtracting fractions with different denominators:

$$\frac{a}{b} + \frac{c}{d} = \frac{ad+bc}{bd} \qquad \frac{a}{b} - \frac{c}{d} = \frac{ad-bc}{bd}$$

Examples:

Example 1. Find the sum. $\frac{2}{3} + \frac{1}{2} =$

Solution: These two fractions are "unlike" fractions. (they have different denominators). Use this formula: $\frac{a}{b} + \frac{c}{d} = \frac{ad+cb}{bd}$

Then: $\frac{2}{3} + \frac{1}{2} = \frac{(2)(2)+(3)(1)}{3 \times 2} = \frac{4+3}{6} = \frac{7}{6}$

Example 2. Find the difference. $\frac{3}{5} - \frac{2}{7} =$

Solution: For "unlike" fractions, find equivalent fractions with the same denominator before you can add or subtract fractions with different denominators. Use this formula: $\frac{a}{b} - \frac{c}{d} = \frac{ad-bc}{bd}$

$\frac{3}{5} - \frac{2}{7} = \frac{(3)(7)-(2)(5)}{5 \times 7} = \frac{21-10}{35} = \frac{11}{35}$

Multiplying and Dividing Fractions

- **Multiplying fractions:** multiply the top numbers and multiply the bottom numbers. Simplify if necessary. $\frac{a}{b} \times \frac{c}{d} = \frac{a \times c}{b \times d}$

- **Dividing fractions:** Keep, Change, Flip

- Keep the first fraction, change the division sign to multiplication, and flip the numerator and denominator of the second fraction. Then, solve!

$$\frac{a}{b} \div \frac{c}{d} = \frac{a}{b} \times \frac{d}{c} = \frac{a \times d}{b \times c}$$

Examples:

Example 1. Multiply. $\frac{2}{3} \times \frac{3}{5} =$

Solution: Multiply the top numbers and multiply the bottom numbers.
$\frac{2}{3} \times \frac{3}{5} = \frac{2 \times 3}{3 \times 5} = \frac{6}{15}$, now, simplify: $\frac{6}{15} = \frac{6 \div 3}{15 \div 3} = \frac{2}{5}$

Example 2. Solve. $\frac{3}{4} \div \frac{2}{5} =$

Solution: Keep the first fraction, change the division sign to multiplication, and flip the numerator and denominator of the second fraction.
Then: $\frac{3}{4} \div \frac{2}{5} = \frac{3}{4} \times \frac{5}{2} = \frac{3 \times 5}{4 \times 2} = \frac{15}{8}$

Example 3. Calculate. $\frac{4}{5} \times \frac{3}{4} =$

Solution: Multiply the top numbers and multiply the bottom numbers.
$\frac{4}{5} \times \frac{3}{4} = \frac{4 \times 3}{5 \times 4} = \frac{12}{20}$, simplify: $\frac{12}{20} = \frac{12 \div 4}{20 \div 4} = \frac{3}{5}$

Example 4. Solve. $\frac{5}{6} \div \frac{3}{7} =$

Solution: Keep the first fraction, change the division sign to multiplication, and flip the numerator and denominator of the second fraction.
Then: $\frac{5}{6} \div \frac{3}{7} = \frac{5}{6} \times \frac{7}{3} = \frac{5 \times 7}{6 \times 3} = \frac{35}{18}$

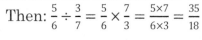

Adding Mixed Numbers

Use the following steps for adding mixed numbers:

- Add whole numbers of the mixed numbers.

- Add the fractions of the mixed numbers.

- Find the Least Common Denominator (LCD) if necessary.

- Add whole numbers and fractions.

- Write your answer in lowest terms.

Examples:

Example 1. Add mixed numbers. $2\frac{1}{2} + 1\frac{2}{3} =$

Solution: Let's rewriting our equation with parts separated, $2\frac{1}{2} + 1\frac{2}{3} = 2 + \frac{1}{2} + 1 + \frac{2}{3}$.
Now, add whole number parts: $2 + 1 = 3$

Add the fraction parts $\frac{1}{2} + \frac{2}{3}$. Rewrite to solve with the equivalent fractions. $\frac{1}{2} + \frac{2}{3} = \frac{3}{6} + \frac{4}{6} = \frac{7}{6}$. The answer is an improper fraction (numerator is bigger than denominator). Convert the improper fraction into a mixed number: $\frac{7}{6} = 1\frac{1}{6}$. Now, combine the whole and fraction parts: $3 + 1\frac{1}{6} = 4\frac{1}{6}$

Example 2. Find the sum. $1\frac{3}{4} + 2\frac{1}{2} =$

Solution: Rewriting our equation with parts separated, $1 + \frac{3}{4} + 2 + \frac{1}{2}$. Add the whole number parts:

$1 + 2 = 3$. Add the fraction parts: $\frac{3}{4} + \frac{1}{2} = \frac{3}{4} + \frac{2}{4} = \frac{5}{4}$

Convert the improper fraction into a mixed number: $\frac{5}{4} = 1\frac{1}{4}$.

Now, combine the whole and fraction parts: $3 + 1\frac{1}{4} = 4\frac{1}{4}$

bit.ly/2M4oABB

Find more at

Subtracting Mixed Numbers

Use these steps for subtracting mixed numbers.

- Convert mixed numbers into improper fractions. $a\frac{c}{b} = \frac{ab+c}{b}$

- Find equivalent fractions with the same denominator for unlike fractions. (fractions with different denominators)

- Subtract the second fraction from the first one. $\frac{a}{b} - \frac{c}{d} = \frac{ad-bc}{bd}$

- Write your answer in lowest terms.

- If the answer is an improper fraction, convert it into a mixed number.

Examples:

Example 1. Subtract. $2\frac{1}{3} - 1\frac{1}{2} =$

Solution: Convert mixed numbers into fractions: $2\frac{1}{3} = \frac{2\times3+1}{3} = \frac{7}{3}$ and $1\frac{1}{2} = \frac{1\times2+1}{2} = \frac{3}{2}$

These two fractions are "unlike" fractions. (they have different denominators).

Find equivalent fractions with the same denominator. Use this formula: $\frac{a}{b} - \frac{c}{d} = \frac{ad-bc}{bd}$

$\frac{7}{3} - \frac{3}{2} = \frac{(7)(2)-(3)(3)}{3\times2} = \frac{14-9}{6} = \frac{5}{6}$

Example 2. Find the difference. $3\frac{4}{7} - 2\frac{3}{4} =$

Solution: Convert mixed numbers into fractions: $3\frac{4}{7} = \frac{3\times7+4}{7} = \frac{25}{7}$ and $2\frac{3}{4} = \frac{2\times4+3}{4} = \frac{11}{4}$

Then: $3\frac{4}{7} - 2\frac{3}{4} = \frac{25}{7} - \frac{11}{4} = \frac{(25)(4)-(11)(7)}{7\times4} = \frac{23}{28}$

Multiplying Mixed Numbers

Use the following steps for multiplying mixed numbers:

- Convert the mixed numbers into fractions. $a\frac{c}{b} = a + \frac{c}{b} = \frac{ab+c}{b}$

- Multiply fractions. $\frac{a}{b} \times \frac{c}{d} = \frac{a \times c}{b \times d}$

- Write your answer in lowest terms.

- If the answer is an improper fraction (numerator is bigger than denominator), convert it into a mixed number.

Examples:

Example 1. Multiply. $4\frac{1}{2} \times 2\frac{2}{5} =$

Solution: Convert mixed numbers into fractions, $4\frac{1}{2} = \frac{4 \times 2 + 1}{2} = \frac{9}{2}$ and $2\frac{2}{5} = \frac{2 \times 5 + 2}{5} = \frac{12}{5}$. Apply the fractions rule for multiplication: $\frac{9}{2} \times \frac{12}{5} = \frac{9 \times 12}{2 \times 5} = \frac{108}{10} = \frac{54}{5}$

The answer is an improper fraction. Convert it into a mixed number. $\frac{54}{5} = 10\frac{4}{5}$

Example 2. Multiply. $3\frac{2}{3} \times 2\frac{5}{6} =$

Solution: Converting mixed numbers into fractions, $3\frac{2}{3} \times 2\frac{5}{6} = \frac{11}{3} \times \frac{17}{6}$

Apply the fractions rule for multiplication: $\frac{11}{3} \times \frac{17}{6} = \frac{11 \times 17}{3 \times 6} = \frac{187}{18} = 10\frac{7}{18}$

Example 3. Find the product. $5\frac{1}{4} \times 3\frac{3}{8} =$

Solution: Convert mixed numbers to fractions: $5\frac{1}{4} = \frac{21}{4}$ and $3\frac{3}{8} = \frac{27}{8}$. Multiply two fractions:

$\frac{21}{4} \times \frac{27}{8} = \frac{21 \times 27}{4 \times 8} = \frac{567}{32} = 17\frac{23}{32}$

bit.ly/3aPy7XJ

Find more at

Dividing Mixed Numbers

Use the following steps for dividing mixed numbers:

- Convert the mixed numbers into fractions. $a\frac{c}{b} = a + \frac{c}{b} = \frac{ab + c}{b}$

- Divide fractions: Keep, Change, Flip: Keep the first fraction, change the division sign to multiplication, and flip the numerator and denominator of the second fraction. Then, solve! $\frac{a}{b} \div \frac{c}{d} = \frac{a}{b} \times \frac{d}{c} = \frac{a \times d}{b \times c}$

- Write your answer in lowest terms.

- If the answer is an improper fraction (numerator is bigger than denominator), convert it into a mixed number.

Examples:

Example 1. Solve. $2\frac{1}{3} \div 1\frac{1}{2}$

Solution: Convert mixed numbers into fractions: $2\frac{1}{3} = \frac{2 \times 3 + 1}{3} = \frac{7}{3}$ and $1\frac{1}{2} = \frac{1 \times 2 + 1}{2} = \frac{3}{2}$
Keep, Change, Flip: $\frac{7}{3} \div \frac{3}{2} = \frac{7}{3} \times \frac{2}{3} = \frac{7 \times 2}{3 \times 3} = \frac{14}{9}$. The answer is an improper fraction.
Convert it into a mixed number: $\frac{14}{9} = 1\frac{5}{9}$

Example 2. Solve. $3\frac{3}{4} \div 2\frac{2}{5}$

Solution: Convert mixed numbers to fractions, then solve:
$3\frac{3}{4} \div 2\frac{2}{5} = \frac{15}{4} \div \frac{12}{5} = \frac{15}{4} \times \frac{5}{12} = \frac{75}{48} = 1\frac{9}{16}$

Example 3. Solve. $2\frac{4}{5} \div 1\frac{2}{3}$

Solution: Converting mixed numbers to fractions: $2\frac{4}{5} \div 1\frac{2}{3} = \frac{14}{5} \div \frac{5}{3}$
Keep, Change, Flip: $\frac{14}{5} \div \frac{5}{3} = \frac{14}{5} \times \frac{3}{5} = \frac{14 \times 3}{5 \times 5} = \frac{42}{25} = 1\frac{17}{25}$

Chapter 1: Practices

✎ Simplify each fraction.

1) $\dfrac{2}{8} =$

2) $\dfrac{5}{15} =$

3) $\dfrac{10}{90} =$

4) $\dfrac{12}{16} =$

5) $\dfrac{25}{45} =$

6) $\dfrac{42}{54} =$

7) $\dfrac{48}{60} =$

8) $\dfrac{52}{169} =$

✎ Find the sum or difference.

9) $\dfrac{3}{10} + \dfrac{2}{10} =$

10) $\dfrac{4}{9} - \dfrac{1}{9} =$

11) $\dfrac{2}{3} + \dfrac{6}{15} =$

12) $\dfrac{17}{24} - \dfrac{5}{8} =$

13) $\dfrac{7}{54} - \dfrac{1}{9} =$

14) $\dfrac{4}{5} - \dfrac{1}{6} =$

15) $\dfrac{6}{7} - \dfrac{3}{8} =$

16) $\dfrac{2}{13} + \dfrac{1}{4} =$

✎ Find the products or quotients.

17) $\dfrac{2}{9} \div \dfrac{4}{3} =$

18) $\dfrac{14}{5} \div \dfrac{28}{35} =$

19) $\dfrac{9}{25} \times \dfrac{5}{27} =$

20) $\dfrac{65}{72} \times \dfrac{12}{15} =$

✎ Find the sum.

21) $2\dfrac{1}{5} + 1\dfrac{2}{5} =$

22) $5\dfrac{1}{9} + 2\dfrac{7}{9} =$

23) $2\dfrac{3}{4} + 1\dfrac{1}{8} =$

24) $2\dfrac{2}{7} + 4\dfrac{1}{21} =$

25) $5\dfrac{3}{5} + 1\dfrac{4}{9} =$

26) $3\dfrac{3}{11} + 4\dfrac{6}{7} =$

Effortless
Math
Education

✎ Find the difference.

27) $5\frac{1}{3} - 4\frac{2}{3} =$

28) $4\frac{7}{10} - 1\frac{3}{10} =$

29) $3\frac{1}{3} - 2\frac{2}{9} =$

30) $6\frac{1}{2} - 3\frac{1}{3} =$

31) $4\frac{3}{4} - 2\frac{1}{28} =$

32) $4\frac{2}{7} - 3\frac{1}{6} =$

33) $5\frac{3}{10} - 3\frac{3}{4} =$

34) $6\frac{9}{20} - 2\frac{1}{3} =$

✎ Find the products.

35) $1\frac{1}{2} \times 2\frac{3}{7} =$

36) $1\frac{3}{4} \times 1\frac{3}{5} =$

37) $4\frac{1}{2} \times 1\frac{5}{6} =$

38) $1\frac{2}{7} \times 3\frac{1}{5} =$

39) $2\frac{1}{5} \times 5\frac{1}{2} =$

40) $2\frac{1}{2} \times 4\frac{4}{5} =$

41) $3\frac{1}{5} \times 4\frac{1}{2} =$

42) $4\frac{9}{10} \times 4\frac{1}{2} =$

✎ Solve.

43) $1\frac{1}{3} \div 1\frac{2}{3} =$

44) $2\frac{1}{4} \div 1\frac{1}{2} =$

45) $5\frac{1}{3} \div 3\frac{1}{2} =$

46) $3\frac{2}{7} \div 1\frac{1}{8} =$

47) $4\frac{1}{5} \div 2\frac{2}{3} =$

48) $1\frac{2}{3} \div 1\frac{3}{8} =$

49) $4\frac{1}{2} \div 2\frac{2}{3} =$

50) $1\frac{2}{11} \div 1\frac{1}{8} =$

Effortless

Math

Education

Chapter 1: Answers

1) $\frac{1}{4}$

2) $\frac{1}{3}$

3) $\frac{1}{9}$

4) $\frac{3}{4}$

5) $\frac{5}{9}$

6) $\frac{7}{9}$

7) $\frac{4}{5}$

8) $\frac{4}{13}$

9) $\frac{1}{2}$

10) $\frac{1}{3}$

11) $\frac{16}{15} = 1\frac{1}{15}$

12) $\frac{1}{12}$

13) $\frac{1}{54}$

14) $\frac{19}{30}$

15) $\frac{27}{56}$

16) $\frac{21}{52}$

17) $\frac{1}{6}$

18) $\frac{7}{2} = 3\frac{1}{2}$

19) $\frac{1}{15}$

20) $\frac{13}{18}$

21) $3\frac{3}{5}$

22) $7\frac{8}{9}$

23) $3\frac{7}{8}$

24) $6\frac{1}{3}$

25) $7\frac{2}{45}$

26) $8\frac{10}{77}$

27) $\frac{2}{3}$

28) $3\frac{2}{5}$

29) $1\frac{1}{9}$

30) $3\frac{1}{6}$

31) $2\frac{5}{7}$

32) $1\frac{5}{42}$

33) $1\frac{11}{20}$

34) $4\frac{7}{60}$

35) $3\frac{9}{14}$

36) $2\frac{4}{5}$

37) $8\frac{1}{4}$

38) $4\frac{4}{35}$

39) $12\frac{1}{10}$

40) 12

41) $14\frac{2}{5}$

42) $22\frac{1}{20}$

43) $\frac{4}{5}$

44) $1\frac{1}{2}$

45) $1\frac{11}{21}$

46) $2\frac{58}{63}$

47) $1\frac{23}{40}$

48) $1\frac{7}{33}$

49) $1\frac{11}{16}$

50) $1\frac{5}{99}$

Effortless

Math

Education

CHAPTER
2 Decimals

Math topics that you'll learn in this chapter:

- ☑ Comparing Decimals
- ☑ Rounding Decimals
- ☑ Adding and Subtracting Decimals
- ☑ Multiplying and Dividing Decimals

13

Comparing Decimals

- A decimal is a fraction written in a special form. For example, instead of writing $\frac{1}{2}$ you can write: 0.5

- A Decimal Number contains a Decimal Point. It separates the whole number part from the fractional part of a decimal number.

- Let's review decimal place values: Example: **45.3861**

4: tens   5: ones   3: tenths

8: hundredths   6: thousandths   1: tens thousandths

- To compare two decimals, compare each digit of two decimals in the same place value. Start from left. Compare hundreds, tens, ones, tenth, hundredth, etc.

- To compare numbers, use these symbols:

Equal to =   Less than <   Greater than >

Greater than or equal ≥   Less than or equal ≤

Examples:

Example 1. Compare 0.03 and 0.30.

Solution: 0.30 *is greater than* 0.03, because the tenth place of 0.30 is 3, but the tenth place of 0.03 is zero. Then: 0.03 < 0.30

Example 2. Compare 0.0917 and 0.217.

Solution: 0.217 *is greater than* 0.0917, because the tenth place of 0.217 is 2, but the tenth place of 0.0917 is zero. Then: 0.0917 < 0.217

Rounding Decimals

- We can round decimals to a certain accuracy or number of decimal places. This is used to make calculations easier to do and results easier to understand when exact values are not too important.

- First, you'll need to remember your place values: For example: **12.4869**

1: tens	2: ones	4: tenths
8: hundredths	6: thousandths	9: tens thousandths

- To round a decimal, first find the place value you'll round to.

- Find the digit to the right of the place value you're rounding to. If it is 5 or bigger, add 1 to the place value you're rounding to and remove all digits on its right side. If the digit to the right of the place value is less than 5, keep the place value and remove all digits on the right.

Examples:

Example 1. Round 4.3679 to the thousandth place value.

Solution: First, look at the next place value to the right, (tens thousandths). It's 9 and it is greater than 5. Thus add 1 to the digit in the thousandth place. The thousandth place is 7. $\rightarrow 7 + 1 = 8$, then, the answer is 4.368

Example 2. Round 1.5237 to the nearest hundredth.

Solution: First, look at the digit to the right of hundredth (thousandths place value). It's 3 and it is less than 5, thus remove all the digits to the right of hundredth place. Then, the answer is 1.52

Find more at bit.ly/3mKEluf

Adding and Subtracting Decimals

- Line up the decimal numbers.

- Add zeros to have the same number of digits for both numbers if necessary.

- Remember your place values: For example: 73.5196

  7: tens   3: ones   5: tenths

  1: hundredths   9: thousandths   6: tens thousandths

- Add or subtract using column addition or subtraction.

Examples:

Example 1. Add. $1.7 + 4.12$

Solution: First, line up the numbers: $\begin{array}{r} 1.7 \\ +\ 4.12 \\ \hline \end{array}$ → Add a zero to have the same number of digits for both numbers. $\begin{array}{r} 1.70 \\ +\ 4.12 \\ \hline \end{array}$ → Start with the hundredths place: $0 + 2 = 2$, $\begin{array}{r} 1.70 \\ +\ 4.12 \\ \hline 2 \end{array}$ → Continue with tenths place: $7 + 1 = 8$, $\begin{array}{r} 1.70 \\ +\ 4.12 \\ \hline .82 \end{array}$ → Add the ones place: $4 + 1 = 5$, $\begin{array}{r} 1.70 \\ +\ 4.12 \\ \hline 5.82 \end{array}$ The answer is 5.82.

Example 2. Find the difference. $5.58 - 4.23$

Solution: First, line up the numbers: $\begin{array}{r} 5.58 \\ -\ 4.23 \\ \hline \end{array}$ → Start with the hundredths place: $8 - 3 = 5$, $\begin{array}{r} 5.58 \\ -\ 4.23 \\ \hline 5 \end{array}$ → Continue with tenths place. $5 - 2 = 3$, $\begin{array}{r} 5.58 \\ -\ 4.23 \\ \hline .35 \end{array}$ → Subtract the ones place. $5 - 4 = 1$, $\begin{array}{r} 5.58 \\ -\ 4.23 \\ \hline 1.35 \end{array}$

Multiplying and Dividing Decimals

For multiplying decimals:

- Ignore the decimal point and set up and multiply the numbers as you do with whole numbers.

- Count the total number of decimal places in both of the factors.

- Place the decimal point in the product.

For dividing decimals:

- If the divisor is not a whole number, move the decimal point to the right to make it a whole number. Do the same for the dividend.

- Divide similar to whole numbers.

Examples:

Example 1. Find the product. $0.65 \times 0.24 =$

Solution: Set up and multiply the numbers as you do with whole numbers. Line up the numbers: $\begin{array}{r} 65 \\ \times 24 \\ \hline \end{array}$ → Start with the ones place then continue with other digits $\rightarrow \begin{array}{r} 65 \\ \times 24 \\ \hline 1,560 \end{array}$. Count the total number of decimal places in both of the factors. There are four decimals digits. (two for each factor 0.65 and 0.24) Then: $0.65 \times 0.24 = 0.1560 = 0.156$

Example 2. Find the quotient. $1.20 \div 0.4 =$

Solution: The divisor is not a whole number. Multiply it by 10 to get 4: → $0.4 \times 10 = 4$
Do the same for the dividend to get 12. → $1.20 \times 10 = 12$
Now, divide $12 \div 4 = 3$. The answer is 3.

Chapter 2: Practices

✎ Compare. Use >, =, and <

1) 0.5 ☐ 0.6

2) 0.9 ☐ 0.8

3) 0.1 ☐ 0.2

4) 0.02 ☐ 0.06

5) 0.05 ☐ 0.08

6) 0.12 ☐ 0.09

7) 3.2 ☐ 2.5

8) 4.8 ☐ 8.4

9) 0.005 ☐ 0.05

10) 2.02 ☐ 20.020

11) 55.100 ☐ 55.10

12) 0.44 ☐ 0.440

13) 6.01 ☐ 6.0100

14) 0.77 ☐ 77.0

✎ Round each decimal to the nearest whole number.

15) 5.8

16) 6.4

17) 12.3

18) 9.2

19) 7.6

20) 22.4

21) 6.8

22) 15.9

23) 13.41

24) 16.78

25) 67.58

26) 42.67

27) 55.89

28) 14.32

29) 78.88

30) 98.29

✎ **Find the sum or difference.**

31) $12.1 + 36.2 =$ 39) $96.23 - 28.32 =$

32) $56.3 - 22.2 =$ 40) $57.33 + 67.46 =$

33) $45.1 + 12.8 =$ 41) $46.26 - 39.49 =$

34) $27.9 - 16.4 =$ 42) $44.95 + 76.53 =$

35) $98.8 - 56.6 =$ 43) $79.37 - 52.89 =$

36) $28.45 + 13.22 =$ 44) $19.99 + 28.7 =$

37) $16.78 + 45.11 =$ 45) $83.48 - 49.3 =$

38) $86.16 - 72.12 =$ 46) $19.6 + 42.98 =$

✎ **Find the product or quotient.**

47) $3.3 \times 0.2 =$ 55) $2.1 \times 8.4 =$

48) $2.4 \div 0.3 =$ 56) $1.6 \times 4.5 =$

49) $8.1 \times 1.4 =$ 57) $9.2 \times 3.1 =$

50) $4.8 \div 0.2 =$ 58) $36.6 \div 1.6 =$

51) $4.1 \times 0.3 =$ 59) $1.91 \times 5.2 =$

52) $8.6 \div 0.2 =$ 60) $3.65 \times 1.4 =$

53) $9.9 \times 0.8 =$ 61) $24.82 \div 0.4 =$

54) $1.84 \div 0.2 =$ 62) $12.4 \times 4.20 =$

Effortless
Math
Education

Chapter 2: Answers

1) <	22) 16	43) 26.48
2) >	23) 13	44) 48.69
3) <	24) 17	45) 34.18
4) <	25) 68	46) 62.58
5) <	26) 43	47) 0.66
6) >	27) 56	48) 8
7) >	28) 14	49) 11.34
8) <	29) 79	50) 24
9) <	30) 98	51) 1.23
10) <	31) 48.3	52) 43
11) =	32) 34.1	53) 7.92
12) =	33) 57.9	54) 9.2
13) =	34) 11.5	55) 17.64
14) <	35) 42.2	56) 7.2
15) 6	36) 41.67	57) 28.52
16) 6	37) 61.89	58) 22.875
17) 12	38) 14.04	59) 9.932
18) 9	39) 67.91	60) 5.11
19) 8	40) 124.79	61) 62.05
20) 22	41) 6.77	62) 52.08
21) 7	42) 121.48	

Effortless
Math
Education

CHAPTER

3

Integers and Order of Operations

Math topics that you'll learn in this chapter:

- ☑ Adding and Subtracting Integers
- ☑ Multiplying and Dividing Integers
- ☑ Order of Operations
- ☑ Integers and Absolute Value

21

Adding and Subtracting Integers

- Integers include zero, counting numbers, and the negative of the counting numbers. $\{\dots, -3, -2, -1, 0, 1, 2, 3, \dots\}$

- Add a positive integer by moving to the right on the number line. (you will get a bigger number)

- Add a negative integer by moving to the left on the number line. (you will get a smaller number)

- Subtract an integer by adding its opposite.

Number line

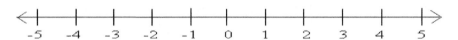

Examples:

Example 1. Solve. $(-2) - (-8) =$

Solution: Keep the first number and convert the sign of the second number to its opposite. (change subtraction into addition. Then: $(-2) + 8 = 6$

Example 2. Solve. $4 + (5 - 10) =$

Solution: First, subtract the numbers in brackets, $5 - 10 = -5$.
Then: $4 + (-5) = \;\rightarrow$ change addition into subtraction: $4 - 5 = -1$

Example 3. Solve. $(9 - 14) + 15 =$

Solution: First, subtract the numbers in brackets, $9 - 14 = -5$
Then: $-5 + 15 = \;\rightarrow -5 + 15 = 10$

Example 4. Solve. $12 + (-3 - 10) =$

Solution: First, subtract the numbers in brackets, $-3 - 10 = -13$
Then: $12 + (-13) = \;\rightarrow$ change addition into subtraction: $12 - 13 = -1$

Multiplying and Dividing Integers

Use the following rules for multiplying and dividing integers:

- (negative) × (negative) = positive

- (negative) ÷ (negative) = positive

- (negative) × (positive) = negative

- (negative) ÷ (positive) = negative

- (positive) × (positive) = positive

- (positive) ÷ (negative) = negative

Examples:

Example 1. Solve. $3 \times (-4) =$

Solution: Use this rule: (positive) × (negative) = negative.
Then: $(3) \times (-4) = -12$

Example 2. Solve. $(-3) + (-24 \div 3) =$

Solution: First, divide -24 by 3, the numbers in brackets, use this rule:
(negative) ÷ (positive) = negative. Then: $-24 \div 3 = -8$
$(-3) + (-24 \div 3) = (-3) + (-8) = -3 - 8 = -11$

Example 3. Solve. $(12 - 15) \times (-2) =$

Solution: First, subtract the numbers in brackets,
$12 - 15 = -3 \rightarrow (-3) \times (-2) =$
Now use this rule: (negative) × (negative) = positive $\rightarrow (-3) \times (-2) = 6$

Example 4. Solve. $(12 - 8) \div (-4) =$

Solution: First, subtract the numbers in brackets,
$12 - 8 = 4 \rightarrow (4) \div (-4) =$
Now use this rule: (positive) ÷ (negative) = negative $\rightarrow (4) \div (-4) =$
-1

Order of Operations

- In Mathematics, "operations" are addition, subtraction, multiplication, division, exponentiation (written as b^n), and grouping.

- When there is more than one math operation in an expression, use PEMDAS: (to memorize this rule, remember the phrase "Please Excuse My Dear Aunt Sally".)

  ❖ Parentheses

  ❖ Exponents

  ❖ Multiplication and Division (from left to right)

  ❖ Addition and Subtraction (from left to right)

Examples:

Example 1. Calculate. $(2 + 6) \div (2^2 \div 4) =$

Solution: First, simplify inside parentheses:
$(8) \div (4 \div 4) = (8) \div (1)$, Then: $(8) \div (1) = 8$

Example 2. Solve. $(6 \times 5) - (14 - 5) =$

Solution: First, calculate within parentheses: $(6 \times 5) - (14 - 5) = (30) - (9)$, Then: $(30) - (9) = 21$

Example 3. Calculate. $-4[(3 \times 6) \div (9 \times 2)] =$

Solution: First, calculate within parentheses:
$-4[(18) \div (9 \times 2)] = -4[(18) \div (18)] = -4[1]$
multiply -4 and 1. Then: $-4[1] = -4$

Example 4. Solve. $(28 \div 7) + (-19 + 3) =$

Solution: First, calculate within parentheses:
$(28 \div 7) + (-19 + 3) = (4) + (-16)$ Then: $(4) - (16) = -12$

Integers and Absolute Value

- The absolute value of a number is its distance from zero, in either direction, on the number line. For example, the distance of 9 and -9 from zero on number line is 9.

- The absolute value of an integer is the numerical value without its sign. (negative or positive)

- The vertical bar is used for absolute value as in $|x|$.

- The absolute value of a number is never negative; because it only shows, "how far the number is from zero".

Examples:

Example 1. Calculate. $|14 - 2| \times 5 =$

Solution: First, solve $|14 - 2|$, $\rightarrow |14 - 2| = |12|$, the absolute value of 12 is 12, $|12| = 12$, Then: $12 \times 5 = 60$

Example 2. Solve. $\frac{|-24|}{4} \times |5 - 7| =$

Solution: First, find $|-24| \rightarrow$ the absolute value of -24 is 24. Then: $|-24| = 24$, $\frac{24}{4} \times |5 - 7| =$

Now, calculate $|5 - 7|$, $\rightarrow |5 - 7| = |-2|$, the absolute value of -2 is 2. $|-2| = 2$ Then: $\frac{24}{4} \times 2 = 6 \times 2 = 12$

Example 3. Solve. $|8 - 2| \times \frac{|-4 \times 7|}{2} =$

Solution: First, calculate $|8 - 2|$, $\rightarrow |8 - 2| = |6|$, the absolute value of 6 is 6, $|6| = 6$. Then: $6 \times \frac{|-4 \times 7|}{2}$

Now calculate $|-4 \times 7|$, $\rightarrow |-4 \times 7| = |-28|$, the absolute value of -28 is 28, $|-28| = 28$, Then: $6 \times \frac{28}{2} = 6 \times 14 = 84$

bit.ly/3aD521u

Find more at

Chapter 3: Practices

✍ Find each sum or difference.

1) $-9 + 16 =$

2) $-18 - 6 =$

3) $-24 + 10 =$

4) $30 + (-5) =$

5) $15 + (-3) =$

6) $(-13) + (-4) =$

7) $25 + (3 - 10) =$

8) $12 - (-6 + 9) =$

9) $5 - (-2 + 7) =$

10) $(-11) + (-5 + 6) =$

11) $(-3) + (9 - 16) =$

12) $(-8) - (13 + 4) =$

13) $(-7 + 9) - 39 =$

14) $(-30 + 6) - 14 =$

15) $(-5 + 9) + (-3 + 7) =$

16) $(8 - 19) - (-4 + 12) =$

17) $(-9 + 2) - (6 - 7) =$

18) $(-12 - 5) - (-4 - 14) =$

✍ Solve.

19) $3 \times (-6) =$

20) $(-32) \div 4 =$

21) $(-5) \times 4 =$

22) $(25) \div (-5) =$

23) $(-72) \div 8 =$

24) $(-2) \times (-6) \times 5 =$

25) $(-2) \times 3 \times (-7) =$

26) $(-1) \times (-3) \times (-5) =$

27) $(-2) \times (-3) \times (-6) =$

28) $(-12 + 3) \times (-5) =$

29) $(-3 + 4) \times (-11) =$

30) $(-9) \times (6 - 5) =$

31) $(-3 - 7) \times (-6) =$

32) $(-7 + 3) \times (-9 + 6) =$

33) $(-15) \div (-17 + 12) =$

34) $(-3 - 2) \times (-9 + 7) =$

35) $(-15 + 31) \div (-2) =$

36) $(-64) \div (-16 + 8) =$

Effortless
Math
Education

Evaluate each expression.

37) $3 + (2 \times 5) =$

38) $(5 \times 4) - 7 =$

39) $(-9 \times 2) + 6 =$

40) $(7 \times 3) - (-5) =$

41) $(-8) + (2 \times 7) =$

42) $(9 - 6) + (3 \times 4) =$

43) $(-19 + 5) + (6 \times 2) =$

44) $(32 \div 4) + (1 - 13) =$

45) $(-36 \div 6) - (12 + 3) =$

46) $(-16 + 5) - (54 \div 9) =$

47) $(-20 + 4) - (35 \div 5) =$

48) $(42 \div 7) + (2 \times 3) =$

49) $(28 \div 4) + (2 \times 6) =$

50) $2[(3 \times 3) - (4 \times 5)] =$

51) $3[(2 \times 8) + (4 \times 3)] =$

52) $2[(9 \times 3) - (6 \times 4)] =$

53) $4[(4 \times 8) \div (4 \times 4)] =$

54) $-5[(10 \times 8) \div (5 \times 8)] =$

 Find the answers.

55) $|-5| + |7 - 10| =$

56) $|-4 + 6| + |-2| =$

57) $|-9| + |1 - 9| =$

58) $|-7| - |8 - 12| =$

59) $|9 - 11| + |8 - 15| =$

60) $|-7 + 10| - |-8 + 3| =$

61) $|-12 + 6| - |3 - 9| =$

62) $5 + |2 - 6| + |3 - 4| =$

63) $-4 + |2 - 6| + |1 - 9| =$

64) $|-6| \times |-7| + |2 - 8| =$

65) $|-12| \times |-3| + |4 - 28| =$

66) $|4 \times (-2)| \times |-9| =$

67) $|-3 \times 2| \times |-5| =$

68) $|3 - 12| - |-3 \times 7| =$

69) $|-9| + |-7 \times 5| =$

70) $|-11| + |-6 \times 4| =$

71) $|-4 \times 2 + 6| \times |-2 \times 8| =$

72) $|-1 \times 5 + 2| \times |-4| =$

Effortless
Math
Education

Chapter 3: Answers

1) 7	25) 42	49) 19
2) −24	26) −15	50) −22
3) −14	27) −36	51) 84
4) 25	28) 45	52) 6
5) 12	29) −11	53) 8
6) −17	30) −9	54) −10
7) 18	31) 60	55) 8
8) 9	32) 12	56) 4
9) 0	33) 3	57) 17
10) −10	34) 10	58) 3
11) −10	35) −8	59) 9
12) −25	36) 8	60) −2
13) −37	37) 13	61) 0
14) −38	38) 13	62) 10
15) 8	39) −12	63) 8
16) −19	40) 26	64) 48
17) −6	41) 6	65) 60
18) 1	42) 15	66) 72
19) −18	43) −2	67) 30
20) −8	44) −4	68) −12
21) −20	45) −21	69) 44
22) −5	46) −17	70) 35
23) −9	47) −23	71) 32
24) 60	48) 12	72) 12

CHAPTER

4 Ratios and Proportions

Math topics that you'll learn in this chapter:

- ☑ Simplifying Ratios
- ☑ Proportional Ratios
- ☑ Similarity and Ratios

29

Simplifying Ratios

- Ratios are used to make comparisons between two numbers.

- Ratios can be written as a fraction, using the word "to", or with a colon. Example: $\frac{3}{4}$ or "3 to 4" or 3:4

- You can calculate equivalent ratios by multiplying or dividing both sides of the ratio by the same number.

Examples:

Example 1. Simplify. $8:2 =$

Solution: Both numbers 8 and 2 are divisible by $2 \Rightarrow 8 \div 2 = 4$, $4 \div 2 = 2$, Then: $8:2 = 4:1$

Example 2. Simplify. $\frac{9}{33} =$

Solution: Both numbers 9 and 33 are divisible by $3 \Rightarrow 33 \div 3 = 11$, $9 \div 3 = 3$, Then: $\frac{9}{33} = \frac{3}{11}$

Example 3. There are 24 students in a class and 10 are girls. Find the ratio of girls to boys in that class.

Solution: Subtract 10 from 24 to find the number of boys in the class. $24 - 10 = 14$. There are 14 boys in the class. So, the ratio of girls to boys is $10:14$. Now, simplify this ratio. Both 14 and 10 are divisible by 2. Then: $14 \div 2 = 7$, and $10 \div 2 = 5$. In the simplest form, this ratio is $5:7$

Example 4. A recipe calls for butter and sugar in the ratio $3:4$. If you're using 9 cups of butter, how many cups of sugar should you use?

Solution: Since you use 9 cups of butter, or 3 times as much, you need to multiply the amount of sugar by 3. Then: $4 \times 3 = 12$. So, you need to use 12 cups of sugar. You can solve this using equivalent fractions: $\frac{3}{4} = \frac{9}{12}$

bit.ly/3nKwq0Z

Find more at

Proportional Ratios

- Two ratios are proportional if they represent the same relationship.

- A proportion means that two ratios are equal. It can be written in two ways: $\dfrac{a}{b} = \dfrac{c}{d}$ $\qquad a : b = c : d$

- The proportion $\dfrac{a}{b} = \dfrac{c}{d}$ can be written as: $a \times d = c \times b$

Examples:

Example 1. Solve this proportion for x. $\qquad \dfrac{2}{5} = \dfrac{6}{x}$

Solution: Use cross multiplication: $\dfrac{2}{5} = \dfrac{6}{x} \Rightarrow 2 \times x = 6 \times 5 \Rightarrow 2x = 30$

Divide both sides by 2 to find x: $x = \dfrac{30}{2} \Rightarrow x = 15$

Example 2. If a box contains red and blue balls in ratio of $3 : 5$ red to blue, how many red balls are there if 45 blue balls are in the box?

Solution: Write a proportion and solve. $\dfrac{3}{5} = \dfrac{x}{45}$

Use cross multiplication: $3 \times 45 = 5 \times x \Rightarrow 135 = 5x$

Divide to find x: $\quad x = \dfrac{135}{5} \Rightarrow x = 27$. There are 27 red balls in the box.

Example 3. Solve this proportion for x. $\qquad \dfrac{4}{9} = \dfrac{16}{x}$

Solution: Use cross multiplication: $\quad \dfrac{4}{9} = \dfrac{16}{x} \Rightarrow 4 \times x = 9 \times 16 \Rightarrow 4x = 144$

Divide to find x: $\quad x = \dfrac{144}{4} \Rightarrow x = 36$

Example 4. Solve this proportion for x. $\dfrac{5}{7} = \dfrac{20}{x}$

Solution: Use cross multiplication: $\quad \dfrac{5}{7} = \dfrac{20}{x} \Rightarrow 5 \times x = 7 \times 20 \Rightarrow 5x = 140$

Divide to find x: $\quad x = \dfrac{140}{5} \Rightarrow x = 28$

bit.ly/37GHQxp

Find more at

Similarity and Ratios

- Two figures are similar if they have the same shape.

- Two or more figures are similar if the corresponding angles are equal, and the corresponding sides are in proportion.

Examples:

Example 1. The following triangles are similar. What is the value of the unknown side?

Solution: Find the corresponding sides and write a proportion.

$\frac{8}{16} = \frac{6}{x}$. Now, use the cross product to solve for x:

$\frac{8}{16} = \frac{6}{x} \rightarrow 8 \times x = 16 \times 6 \rightarrow 8x = 96$. Divide both sides by 8. Then: $8x = 96 \rightarrow x = \frac{96}{8} \rightarrow x = 12$

The missing side is 12.

Example 2. Two rectangles are similar. The first is 5 feet wide and 15 feet long. The second is 10 feet wide. What is the length of the second rectangle?

Solution: Let's put x for the length of the second rectangle. Since two rectangles are similar, their corresponding sides are in proportion. Write a proportion and solve for the missing number.

$$\frac{5}{10} = \frac{15}{x} \rightarrow 5x = 10 \times 15 \rightarrow 5x = 150 \rightarrow x = \frac{150}{5} = 30$$

The length of the second rectangle is 30 feet.

Chapter 4: Practices

✍ Reduce each ratio.

1) $2 : 18 =$ ___ : ___

2) $5 : 35 =$ ___ : ___

3) $8 : 72 =$ ___ : ___

4) $24 : 36 =$ ___ : ___

5) $25 : 40 =$ ___ : ___

6) $40 : 72 =$ ___ : ___

7) $28 : 63 =$ ___ : ___

8) $18 : 81 =$ ___ : ___

9) $13 : 52 =$ ___ : ___

10) $56 : 72 =$ ___ : ___

11) $42 : 63 =$ ___ : ___

12) $32 : 96 =$ ___ : ___

✍ Solve.

13) Bob has 16 red cards and 20 green cards. What is the ratio of Bob's red cards to his green cards? _____

14) In a party, 34 soft drinks are required for every 20 guests. If there are 260 guests, how many soft drinks are required? _____

15) Sara has 56 blue pens and 28 black pens. What is the ratio of Sara's black pens to her blue pens? _____

16) In Jack's class, 48 of the students are tall and 20 are short. In Michael's class 28 students are tall and 12 students are short. Which class has a higher ratio of tall to short students? _____

17) The price of 6 apples at the Quick Market is $1.52. The price of 5 of the same apples at Walmart is $1.32. Which place is the better buy? _____

18) The bakers at a Bakery can make 180 bagels in 6 hours. How many bagels can they bake in 16 hours? What is that rate per hour? _____

19) You can buy 6 cans of green beans at a supermarket for $3.48. How much does it cost to buy 38 cans of green beans? _____

Effortless Math Education

✎ Solve each proportion.

20) $\frac{3}{2} = \frac{9}{x} \Rightarrow x = $ ____

21) $\frac{7}{2} = \frac{x}{4} \Rightarrow x = $ ____

22) $\frac{1}{3} = \frac{2}{x} \Rightarrow x = $ ____

23) $\frac{1}{4} = \frac{5}{x} \Rightarrow x = $ ____

24) $\frac{9}{6} = \frac{x}{2} \Rightarrow x = $ ____

25) $\frac{3}{6} = \frac{5}{x} \Rightarrow x = $ ____

26) $\frac{7}{x} = \frac{2}{6} \Rightarrow x = $ ____

27) $\frac{2}{x} = \frac{4}{10} \Rightarrow x = $ ____

28) $\frac{3}{2} = \frac{x}{8} \Rightarrow x = $ ____

29) $\frac{x}{6} = \frac{5}{3} \Rightarrow x = $ ____

30) $\frac{3}{9} = \frac{5}{x} \Rightarrow x = $ ____

31) $\frac{4}{18} = \frac{2}{x} \Rightarrow x = $ ____

32) $\frac{6}{16} = \frac{3}{x} \Rightarrow x = $ ____

33) $\frac{2}{5} = \frac{x}{20} \Rightarrow x = $ ____

34) $\frac{28}{8} = \frac{x}{2} \Rightarrow x = $ ____

35) $\frac{3}{5} = \frac{x}{15} \Rightarrow x = $ ____

36) $\frac{2}{7} = \frac{x}{14} \Rightarrow x = $ ____

37) $\frac{x}{18} = \frac{3}{2} \Rightarrow x = $ ____

38) $\frac{x}{24} = \frac{2}{6} \Rightarrow x = $ ____

39) $\frac{5}{x} = \frac{4}{20} \Rightarrow x = $ ____

40) $\frac{10}{x} = \frac{20}{80} \Rightarrow x = $ ____

41) $\frac{90}{6} = \frac{x}{2} \Rightarrow x = $ ____

✎ Solve each problem.

42) Two rectangles are similar. The first is 8 *feet* wide and 32 *feet* long. The second is 12 *feet* wide. What is the length of the second rectangle?

_____

43) Two rectangles are similar. One is 4.6 *meters* by 7 *meters*. The longer side of the second rectangle is 28 *meters*. What is the other side of the second rectangle? _____

Chapter 4: Answers

1) 1 : 9
2) 1 : 7
3) 1 : 9
4) 2 : 3
5) 5 : 8
6) 5 : 9
7) 4 : 9
8) 2 : 9

9) 1 : 4
10) 7 : 9
11) 2 : 3
12) 1 : 3
13) 4 : 5
14) 442
15) 1 : 2

16) *Jack's class*: $\frac{48}{20} = \frac{12}{5}$ *Michael's class*: $\frac{28}{12} = \frac{7}{3}$ Jack's class has a higher ratio of tall to short student: $\frac{12}{5} > \frac{7}{3}$

17) Quick market
18) 480, 30 bagels per hour
19) $22.04
20) 6
21) 14
22) 6
23) 20
24) 3
25) 10
26) 21
27) 5
28) 12
29) 10
30) 15

31) 9
32) 8
33) 8
34) 7
35) 9
36) 4
37) 27
38) 8
39) 25
40) 40
41) 30
42) 48 *feet*
43) 18.4 *meters*

Effortless
Math
Education

CHAPTER

5 Percentage

Math topics that you'll learn in this chapter:

- ☑ Percent Problems
- ☑ Percent of Increase and Decrease
- ☑ Discount, Tax and Tip
- ☑ Simple Interest

37

Percent Problems

- Percent is a ratio of a number and 100. It always has the same denominator, 100. The percent symbol is "%".

- Percent means "per 100". So, 20% is $\frac{20}{100}$.

- In each percent problem, we are looking for the base, or the part or the percent.

- Use these equations to find each missing section in a percent problem:

  ❖ Base = Part ÷ Percent

  ❖ Part = Percent × Base

  ❖ Percent = Part ÷ Base

Examples:

Example 1. What is 20% of 40?

Solution: In this problem, we have the percent (20%) and the base (40) and we are looking for the "part". Use this formula: *Part = Percent × Base*.
Then: $Part = 20\% \times 40 = \frac{20}{100} \times 40 = 0.20 \times 40 = 8$. The answer: 20% of 40 is 8.

Example 2. 25 is what percent of 500?

Solution: In this problem, we are looking for the percent. Use this equation:
$Percent = Part \div Base \rightarrow Percent = 25 \div 500 = 0.05 = 5\%$.
Then: 25 is 5 percent of 500.

Example 3. 80 is 20 percent of what number?

Solution: In this problem, we are looking for the base. Use this equation:
$Base = Part \div Percent \rightarrow Base = 80 \div 20\% = 80 \div 0.20 = 400$
Then: 80 is 20 percent of 400.

bit.ly/34Gy3FL

Find more at

Percent of Increase and Decrease

- Percent of change (increase or decrease) is a mathematical concept that represents the degree of change over time.

- To find the percentage of increase or decrease:

  1. New Number – Original Number

  2. (The result ÷ Original Number) × 100

- Or use this formula: Percent of change $= \frac{new\ number - original\ number}{original\ number} \times 100$

- Note: If your answer is a negative number, then this is a percentage decrease. If it is positive, then this is a percentage increase.

Examples:

Example 1. The price of a shirt increases from $30 to $36. What is the percentage increase?

Solution: First, find the difference: $36 - 30 = 6$

Then: $(6 \div 30) \times 100 = \frac{6}{30} \times 100 = 20$. The percentage increase is 20%. It means that the price of the shirt increased by 20%.

Example 2. The price of a table decreased from $50 to $35. What is the percent of decrease?

Solution: Use this formula:

$$Percent\ of\ change = \frac{new\ number - original\ number}{original\ number} \times 100 =$$

$\frac{35-50}{50} \times 100 = \frac{-15}{50} \times 100 = -30$. The percentage decrease is 30. (the negative sign means percentage decrease) Therefore, the price of the table decreased by 30%.

Discount, Tax and Tip

- To find the discount: Multiply the regular price by the rate of discount

- To find the selling price: Original price − discount

- To find tax: Multiply the tax rate to the taxable amount (income, property value, etc.)

- To find the tip, multiply the rate to the selling price.

Examples:

Example 1. With an 20% discount, Ella saved $50 on a dress. What was the original price of the dress?

Solution: let x be the original price of the dress. Then: 20 % *of* $x = 50$. Write an equation and solve for x: $0.20 \times x = 50 \rightarrow x = \frac{50}{0.20} = 250$. The original price of the dress was $250.

Example 2. Sophia purchased a new computer for a price of $820 at the Apple Store. What is the total amount her credit card is charged if the sales tax is 5%?

Solution: The taxable amount is $820, and the tax rate is 5%. Then:
$$Tax = 0.05 \times 820 = 41$$
$$Final\ price = Selling\ price + Tax \rightarrow final\ price = \$820 + \$41 = \$861$$

Example 3. Nicole and her friends went out to eat at a restaurant. If their bill was $60.00 and they gave their server a 15% tip, how much did they pay altogether?

Solution: First, find the tip. To find the tip, multiply the rate to the bill amount. $Tip = 60 \times 0.15 = 9$. The final price is: $60 + $9 = $69

bit.ly/2Je5lo0

Find more at

Simple Interest

- Simple Interest: The charge for borrowing money or the return for lending it.

- Simple interest is calculated on the initial amount (principal).

- To solve a simple interest problem, use this formula:

$Interest = principal \times rate \times time \quad (I = p \times r \times t = prt)$

Examples:

Example 1. Find simple interest for $200 investment at 5% for 3 years.

Solution: Use Interest formula:
$I = prt$ ($P = \$200$, $r = 5\% = \frac{5}{100} = 0.05$ and $t = 3$)
Then: $I = 200 \times 0.05 \times 3 = \$30$

Example 2. Find simple interest for $1,200 at 8% for 6 years.

Solution: Use Interest formula:
$I = prt$ ($P = \$1,200$, $r = 8\% = \frac{8}{100} = 0.08$ and $t = 6$)
Then: $I = 1,200 \times 0.08 \times 6 = \$576$

Example 3. Andy received a student loan to pay for his educational expenses this year. What is the interest on the loan if he borrowed $4,500 at 6% for 5 years?

Solution: Use Interest formula: $I = prt$. $P = \$4,500$, r $= 6\% = 0.06$ and $t = 5$
Then: $I = 4,500 \times 0.06 \times 5 = \$1,350$

Example 4. Bob is starting his own small business. He borrowed $20,000 from the bank at an 8% rate for 6 months. Find the interest Bob will pay on this loan.

Solution: Use Interest formula:
$I = prt$. $P = \$20,000$, $r = 8\% = 0.08$ and $t = 0.5$ (6 months is half year). Then:
$$I = 20,000 \times 0.08 \times 0.5 = \$800$$

Chapter 5: Practices

✎ Solve each problem.

1) What is 15% of 60? ____%

2) What is 55% of 800? ____%

3) What is 22% of 120? ____%

4) What is 18% of 40? ____%

5) 90 is what percent of 200? ____%

6) 30 is what percent of 150? ____%

7) 14 is what percent of 250? ____%

8) 60 is what percent of 300? ____%

9) 30 is 120 percent of what number? ____%

10) 120 is 20 percent of what number? ____%

11) 15 is 5 percent of what number? ____%

12) 22 is 20% of what number? ____%

✎ Solve each problem.

13) Bob got a raise, and his hourly wage increased from $15 to $21. What is the percent increase? _____ %

14) The price of a pair of shoes increases from $32 to $36. What is the percent increase? ___ %

15) At a coffeeshop, the price of a cup of coffee increased from $1.35 to $1.62. What is the percent increase in the cost of the coffee? _____ %

16) A $45 shirt now selling for $36 is discounted by what percent? _____ %

17) Joe scored 30 out of 35 marks in Algebra, 20 out of 30 marks in science and 58 out of 70 marks in mathematics. In which subject his percentage of marks is best? _____

18) Emma purchased a computer for $420. The computer is regularly priced at $480. What was the percent discount Emma received on the computer? _____

19) A chemical solution contains 15% alcohol. If there is 54 ml of alcohol, what is the volume of the solution? _____

Effortless Math Education

✎ Find the selling price of each item.

20) Original price of a computer: $600

   Tax: 8%, Selling price: $_____

21) Original price of a laptop: $450

   Tax: 10%, Selling price: $_____

22) Nicolas hired a moving company. The company charged $500 for its services, and Nicolas gives the movers a 14% tip. How much does Nicolas tip the movers? $_____

23) Mason has lunch at a restaurant and the cost of his meal is $40. Mason wants to leave a 20% tip. What is Mason's total bill, including tip? $_____

✎ Determine the simple interest for the following loans.

24) $1,000 *at* 5% *for* 4 *years.* $__

25) $400 *at* 3% *for* 5 *years.* $__

26) $240 *at* 4% *for* 3 *years.* $__

27) $500 at 4.5% for 6 years. $__

✎ Solve.

28) A new car, valued at $20,000, depreciates at 8% per year. What is the value of the car one year after purchase? $_____

29) Sara puts $7,000 into an investment yielding 3% annual simple interest; she left the money in for five years. How much interest does Sara get at the end of those five years? $_____

| Effortless |
| Math |
| Education |

Chapter 5: Answers

1) 4

2) 440

3) 26.4

4) 7.2

5) 45%

6) 20%

7) 5.6%

8) 20%

9) 25

10) 600

11) 300

12) 110

13) 40%

14) 12.5%

15) 20%

16) 20%

17) Algebra

18) 12.5%

19) 360 ml

20) $648.00

21) $495.00

22) $70.00

23) $48.00

24) $200.00

25) $60.00

26) $28.80

27) $135.00

28) $18.400

29) $1,050

CHAPTER

6 Exponents and Variables

Math topics that you'll learn in this chapter:

- ☑ Multiplication Property of Exponents
- ☑ Division Property of Exponents
- ☑ Powers of Products and Quotients
- ☑ Zero and Negative Exponents
- ☑ Negative Exponents and Negative Bases
- ☑ Scientific Notation
- ☑ Radicals

45

Multiplication Property of Exponents

- Exponents are shorthand for repeated multiplication of the same number by itself. For example, instead of 2×2, we can write 2^2. For $3 \times 3 \times 3 \times 3$, we can write 3^4

- In algebra, a variable is a letter used to stand for a number. The most common letters are: $x, y, z, a, b, c, m,$ and n.

- Exponent's rules: $x^a \times x^b = x^{a+b}$, $\dfrac{x^a}{x^b} = x^{a-b}$

$$(x^a)^b = x^{a \times b} \qquad (xy)^a = x^a \times y^a \qquad \left(\dfrac{a}{b}\right)^c = \dfrac{a^c}{b^c}$$

Examples:

Example 1. Multiply. $2x^2 \times 3x^4$

Solution: Use Exponent's rules: $x^a \times x^b = x^{a+b} \rightarrow x^2 \times x^4 = x^{2+4} = x^6$
Then: $2x^2 \times 3x^4 = 6x^6$

Example 2. Simplify. $(x^4 y^2)^2$

Solution: Use Exponent's rules: $(x^a)^b = x^{a \times b}$.
Then: $(x^4 y^2)^2 = x^{4 \times 2} y^{2 \times 2} = x^8 y^4$

Example 3. Multiply. $5x^8 \times 6x^5$

Solution: Use Exponent's rules: $x^a \times x^b = x^{a+b} \rightarrow x^8 \times x^5 = x^{8+5} = x^{13}$
Then: $5x^8 \times 6x^5 = 30x^{13}$

Example 4. Simplify. $(x^4 y^7)^3$

Solution: Use Exponent's rules: $(x^a)^b = x^{a \times b}$.
Then: $(x^4 y^7)^3 = x^{4 \times 3} y^{7 \times 3} = x^{12} y^{21}$

bit.ly/34AWHr1
Find more at

Division Property of Exponents

For division of exponents use following formulas:

- $\frac{x^a}{x^b} = x^{a-b} \ (x \neq 0)$

- $\frac{x^a}{x^b} = \frac{1}{x^{b-a}}, \ (x \neq 0)$

- $\frac{1}{x^b} = x^{-b}$

Examples:

Example 1. Simplify. $\frac{16x^3y}{2xy^2} =$

Solution: First, cancel the common factor: $2 \rightarrow \frac{16x^3y}{2xy^2} = \frac{8x^3y}{xy^2}$

Use Exponent's rules: $\frac{x^a}{x^b} = x^{a-b} \rightarrow \frac{x^3}{x} = x^{3-1} = x^2$ and $\frac{x^a}{x^b} = \frac{1}{x^{b-a}} \rightarrow \frac{y}{y^2} = \frac{1}{y^{2-1}} = \frac{1}{y}$

Then: $\frac{16x^3y}{2xy^2} = \frac{8x^2}{y}$

Example 2. Simplify. $\frac{24x^8}{3x^6} =$

Solution: Use Exponent's rules: $\frac{x^a}{x^b} = x^{a-b} \rightarrow \frac{x^8}{x^6} = x^{8-6} = x^2$

Then: $\frac{24x^8}{3x^6} = 8x^2$

Example 3. Simplify. $\frac{7x^4y^2}{28x^3y} =$

Solution: First, cancel the common factor: $7 \rightarrow \frac{x^4y^2}{4x^3y}$

Use Exponent's rules: $\frac{x^a}{x^b} = x^{a-b} \rightarrow \frac{x^4}{x^3} = x^{4-3} = x$ and $\frac{y^2}{y} = y$

Then: $\frac{7x^4y^2}{28x^3y} = \frac{xy}{4}$

Powers of Products and Quotients

- For any nonzero numbers a and b and any integer x, $(ab)^x = a^x \times b^x$ and $\left(\frac{a}{b}\right)^c = \frac{a^c}{b^c}$

Examples:

Example 1. Simplify. $(3x^3y^2)^2$

Solution: Use Exponent's rules: $(x^a)^b = x^{a \times b}$

$(3x^3y^2)^2 = (3)^2(x^3)^2(y^2)^2 = 9x^{3 \times 2}y^{2 \times 2} = 9x^6y^4$

Example 2. Simplify. $\left(\frac{2x^3}{3x^2}\right)^2$

Solution: First, cancel the common factor: $x \rightarrow \left(\frac{2x^3}{3x^2}\right) = \left(\frac{2x}{3}\right)^2$

Use Exponent's rules: $\left(\frac{a}{b}\right)^c = \frac{a^c}{b^c}$, Then: $\left(\frac{2x}{3}\right)^2 = \frac{(2x)^2}{(3)^2} = \frac{4x^2}{9}$

Example 3. Simplify. $\left(-4x^3y^5\right)^2$

Solution: Use Exponent's rules: $(x^a)^b = x^{a \times b}$

$$\left(-4x^3y^5\right)^2 = (-4)^2(x^3)^2\left(y^5\right)^2 = 16x^{3 \times 2}y^{5 \times 2} = 16x^6y^{10}$$

Example 4. Simplify. $\left(\frac{5x}{4x^2}\right)^2$

Solution: First, cancel the common factor: $x \rightarrow \left(\frac{5x}{4x^2}\right)^2 = \left(\frac{5}{4x}\right)^2$

Use Exponent's rules: $\left(\frac{a}{b}\right)^c = \frac{a^c}{b^c}$, Then: $\left(\frac{5}{4x}\right)^2 = \frac{5^2}{(4x)^2} = \frac{25}{16x^2}$

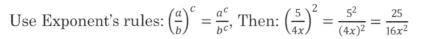

Zero and Negative Exponents

- Zero-Exponent Rule: $a^0 = 1$, this means that anything raised to the zero power is 1. For example: $(5xy)^0 = 1$ (number zero is an exception: $\mathbf{0^0 = 0}$)

- A negative exponent simply means that the base is on the wrong side of the fraction line, so you need to flip the base to the other side. For instance, "x^{-2}" (pronounced as "ecks to the minus two") just means "x^2" but underneath, as in $\frac{1}{x^2}$.

Examples:

Example 1. Evaluate. $\left(\frac{4}{5}\right)^{-2} =$

Solution: Use negative exponent's rule: $\left(\frac{x^a}{x^b}\right)^{-2} = \left(\frac{x^b}{x^a}\right)^2 \rightarrow \left(\frac{4}{5}\right)^{-2} = \left(\frac{5}{4}\right)^2$
Then: $\left(\frac{5}{4}\right)^2 = \frac{5^2}{4^2} = \frac{25}{16}$

Example 2. Evaluate. $\left(\frac{3}{2}\right)^{-3} =$

Solution: Use negative exponent's rule: $\left(\frac{x^a}{x^b}\right)^{-3} = \left(\frac{x^b}{x^a}\right)^3 \rightarrow \left(\frac{3}{2}\right)^{-3} = \left(\frac{2}{3}\right)^3 =$
Then: $\left(\frac{2}{3}\right)^3 = \frac{2^3}{3^3} = \frac{8}{27}$

Example 3. Evaluate. $\left(\frac{a}{b}\right)^0 =$

Solution: Use zero-exponent Rule: $a^0 = 1$
Then: $\left(\frac{a}{b}\right)^0 = 1$

Example 4. Evaluate. $\left(\frac{4}{7}\right)^{-1} =$

Solution: Use negative exponent's rule: $\left(\frac{x^a}{x^b}\right)^{-1} = \left(\frac{x^b}{x^a}\right)^1 \rightarrow \left(\frac{4}{7}\right)^{-1} =$
$\left(\frac{7}{4}\right)^1 = \frac{7}{4}$

Negative Exponents and Negative Bases

- A negative exponent is the reciprocal of that number with a positive exponent. $(3)^{-2} = \frac{1}{3^2}$

- To simplify a negative exponent, make the power positive!

- The parenthesis is important! -5^{-2} is not the same as $(-5)^{-2}$

$$-5^{-2} = -\frac{1}{5^2} \text{ and } (-5)^{-2} = +\frac{1}{5^2}$$

Examples:

Example 1. Simplify. $\left(\frac{2a}{3c}\right)^{-2} =$

Solution: Use negative exponent's rule: $\left(\frac{x^a}{x^b}\right)^{-2} = \left(\frac{x^b}{x^a}\right)^2 \rightarrow \left(\frac{2a}{3c}\right)^{-2} = \left(\frac{3c}{2a}\right)^2$

Now use exponent's rule: $\left(\frac{a}{b}\right)^c = \frac{a^c}{b^c} \rightarrow = \left(\frac{3c}{2a}\right)^2 = \frac{3^2 c^2}{2^2 a^2}$

Then: $\frac{3^2 c^2}{2^2 a^2} = \frac{9c^2}{4a^2}$

Example 2. Simplify. $\left(\frac{x}{4y}\right)^{-3} =$

Solution: Use negative exponent's rule: $\left(\frac{x^a}{x^b}\right)^{-3} = \left(\frac{x^b}{x^a}\right)^3 \rightarrow \left(\frac{x}{4y}\right)^{-3} = \left(\frac{4y}{x}\right)^3$

Now use exponent's rule: $\left(\frac{a}{b}\right)^c = \frac{a^c}{b^c} \rightarrow \left(\frac{4y}{x}\right)^3 = \frac{4^3 y^3}{x^3} = \frac{64y^3}{x^3}$

Example 3. Simplify. $\left(\frac{5a}{2c}\right)^{-2} =$

Solution: Use negative exponent's rule: $\left(\frac{x^a}{x^b}\right)^{-2} = \left(\frac{x^b}{x^a}\right)^2 \rightarrow \left(\frac{5a}{2c}\right)^{-2} = \left(\frac{2c}{5a}\right)^2$

Now use exponent's rule: $\left(\frac{a}{b}\right)^c = \frac{a^c}{b^c} \rightarrow = \left(\frac{2c}{5a}\right)^2 = \frac{2^2 c^2}{5^2 a^2}$

Then: $\frac{2^2 c^2}{5^2 a^2} = \frac{4c^2}{25a^2}$

Scientific Notation

- Scientific notation is used to write very big or very small numbers in decimal form.

- In scientific notation, all numbers are written in the form of: $m \times 10^n$, where m is greater than 1 and less than 10.

- To convert a number from scientific notation to standard form, move the decimal point to the left (if the exponent of ten is a negative number), or to the right (if the exponent is positive).

Examples:

Example 1. Write 0.00024 in scientific notation.

Solution: First, move the decimal point to the right so you have a number between 1 and 10. That number is 2.4. Now, determine how many places the decimal moved in step 1 by the power of 10. We moved the decimal point 4 digits to the right. Then: $10^{-4} \to$ When the decimal moved to the right, the exponent is negative. Then: $0.00024 = 2.4 \times 10^{-4}$

Example 2. Write 3.8×10^{-5} in standard notation.

Solution: The exponent is negative 5. Then, move the decimal point to the left five digits. (remember $3.8 = 0000003.8$) When the decimal moved to the right, the exponent is negative. Then: $3.8 \times 10^{-5} = 0.000038$

Example 3. Write 0.00031 in scientific notation.

Solution: First, move the decimal point to the right so you have a number between 1 and 10. Then: $m = 3.1$, Now, determine how many places the decimal moved in step 1 by the power of 10. $10^{-4} \to$ Then: $0.00031 = 3.1 \times 10^{-4}$

Example 4. Write 6.2×10^5 in standard notation.

Solution: $10^5 \to$ The exponent is positive 5. Then, move the decimal point to the right five digits. (remember $6.2 = 6.20000$) Then: $6.2 \times 10^5 = 620,000$

bit.ly/3nOwJYP

Find more at

Radicals

- If n is a positive integer and x is a real number, then: $\sqrt[n]{x} = x^{\frac{1}{n}}$,

$$\sqrt[n]{xy} = x^{\frac{1}{n}} \times y^{\frac{1}{n}}, \sqrt[n]{\frac{x}{y}} = \frac{x^{\frac{1}{n}}}{y^{\frac{1}{n}}}, \text{ and } \sqrt[n]{x} \times \sqrt[n]{y} = \sqrt[n]{xy}$$

- A square root of x is a number r whose square is: $r^2 = x$ (r is a square root of x)

- To add and subtract radicals, we need to have the same values under the radical. For example: $\sqrt{3} + \sqrt{3} = 2\sqrt{3}, 3\sqrt{5} - \sqrt{5} = 2\sqrt{5}$

Examples:

Example 1. Find the square root of $\sqrt{121}$.

Solution: First, factor the number: $121 = 11^2$, Then: $\sqrt{121} = \sqrt{11^2}$,
Now use radical rule: $\sqrt[n]{a^n} = a$. Then: $\sqrt{121} = \sqrt{11^2} = 11$

Example 2. Evaluate. $\sqrt{4} \times \sqrt{16} =$

Solution: Find the values of $\sqrt{4}$ and $\sqrt{16}$. Then: $\sqrt{4} \times \sqrt{16} = 2 \times 4 = 8$

Example 3. Solve. $5\sqrt{2} + 9\sqrt{2}$.

Solution: Since we have the same values under the radical, we can add these two radicals: $5\sqrt{2} + 9\sqrt{2} = 14\sqrt{2}$

Example 4. Evaluate. $\sqrt{2} \times \sqrt{50} =$

Solution: Use this radical rule: $\sqrt[n]{x} \times \sqrt[n]{y} = \sqrt[n]{xy} \rightarrow \sqrt{2} \times \sqrt{50} = \sqrt{100}$
The square root of 100 is 10. Then: $\sqrt{2} \times \sqrt{50} = \sqrt{100} = 10$

Chapter 6: Practices

✎ Find the products.

1) $x^2 \times 4xy^2 =$

2) $3x^2y \times 5x^3y^2 =$

3) $6x^4y^2 \times x^2y^3 =$

4) $7xy^3 \times 2x^2y =$

5) $-5x^5y^5 \times x^3y^2 =$

6) $-8x^3y^2 \times 3x^3y^2 =$

7) $-6x^2y^6 \times 5x^4y^2 =$

8) $-3x^3y^3 \times 2x^3y^2 =$

9) $-6x^5y^3 \times 4x^4y^3 =$

10) $-2x^4y^3 \times 5x^6y^2 =$

11) $-7y^6 \times 3x^6y^3 =$

12) $-9x^4 \times 2x^4y^2 =$

✎ Simplify.

13) $\frac{5^3 \times 5^4}{5^9 \times 5} =$

14) $\frac{3^3 \times 3^2}{7^2 \times 7} =$

15) $\frac{15x^5}{5x^3} =$

16) $\frac{16x^3}{4x^5} =$

17) $\frac{72y^2}{8x^3y^6} =$

18) $\frac{10x^3y^4}{50x^2y^3} =$

19) $\frac{13y^2}{52x^4y^4} =$

20) $\frac{50xy^3}{200x^3y^4} =$

21) $\frac{48x^2}{56x^2y^2} =$

22) $\frac{81y^6x}{54x^4y^3} =$

✎ Solve.

23) $(x^3y^3)^2 =$

24) $(3x^3y^4)^3 =$

25) $(4x \times 6xy^3)^2 =$

26) $(5x \times 2y^3)^3 =$

27) $\left(\frac{9x}{x^3}\right)^2 =$

28) $\left(\frac{3y}{18y^2}\right)^2 =$

29) $\left(\frac{3x^2y^3}{24x^4y^2}\right)^3 =$

30) $\left(\frac{26x^5y^3}{52x^3y^5}\right)^2 =$

31) $\left(\frac{18x^7y^4}{72x^5y^2}\right)^2 =$

32) $\left(\frac{12x^6y^4}{48x^5y^3}\right)^2 =$

Effortless Math Education

✍ **Evaluate each expression. (Zero and Negative Exponents)**

33) $\left(\frac{1}{4}\right)^{-2} =$

34) $\left(\frac{1}{3}\right)^{-2} =$

35) $\left(\frac{1}{7}\right)^{-3} =$

36) $\left(\frac{2}{5}\right)^{-3} =$

37) $\left(\frac{2}{3}\right)^{-3} =$

38) $\left(\frac{3}{5}\right)^{-4} =$

✍ **Write each expression with positive exponents.**

39) $x^{-7} =$

40) $3y^{-5} =$

41) $15y^{-3} =$

42) $-20x^{-4} =$

43) $12a^{-3}b^5 =$

44) $25a^3b^{-4}c^{-3} =$

45) $-4x^5y^{-3}z^{-6} =$

46) $\frac{18y}{x^3y^{-2}} =$

47) $\frac{20a^{-2}b}{-12c^{-4}}$

✍ **Write each number in scientific notation.**

48) $0.00412 =$

49) $0.000053 =$

50) $66,000 =$

51) $72,000,000 =$

✍ **Evaluate.**

52) $\sqrt{8} \times \sqrt{8} =$ ....

53) $\sqrt{36} - \sqrt{9} =$ ....

54) $\sqrt{81} + \sqrt{16} =$ ....

55) $\sqrt{4} \times \sqrt{25} =$ ....

56) $\sqrt{2} \times \sqrt{32} =$ ....

57) $4\sqrt{3} + 5\sqrt{3} =$ ....

Chapter 6: Answers

1) $4x^3y^2$

2) $15x^5y^3$

3) $6x^6y^5$

4) $14x^3y^4$

5) $-5x^8y^7$

6) $-24x^6y^4$

7) $-30x^6y^8$

8) $-6x^6y^5$

9) $-24x^9y^6$

10) $-10x^{10}y^5$

11) $-21x^6y^9$

12) $-18x^8y^2$

13) $\frac{1}{125}$

14) $\frac{243}{343}$

15) $3x^2$

16) $\frac{4}{x^2}$

17) $\frac{9}{x^3y^4}$

18) $\frac{xy}{5}$

19) $\frac{1}{4x^4y^2}$

20) $\frac{1}{4x^2y}$

21) $\frac{6}{7y^2}$

22) $\frac{3y^3}{2x^3}$

23) x^6y^6

24) $27x^9y^{12}$

25) $576x^4y^6$

26) $1,000x^3y^9$

27) $\frac{81}{x^4}$

28) $\frac{1}{36y^2}$

29) $\frac{y^3}{512x^6}$

30) $\frac{x^4}{4y^4}$

31) $\frac{x^4y^4}{16}$

32) $\frac{x^2y^2}{16}$

33) 16

34) 9

35) 343

36) $\frac{125}{8}$

37) $\frac{27}{8}$

38) $\frac{625}{81}$

39) $\frac{1}{x^7}$

40) $\frac{3}{y^5}$

41) $\frac{15}{y^3}$

42) $-\frac{20}{x^4}$

43) $\frac{12b^5}{a^3}$

44) $\frac{25a^3}{b^4c^3}$

45) $-\frac{4x^5}{y^3z^6}$

46) $\frac{18y^3}{x^3}$

47) $-\frac{5bc^4}{3a^2}$

48) 4.12×10^{-3}

49) 5.3×10^{-5}

50) 6.6×10^4

51) 7.2×10^7

52) 8

53) 3

54) 13

55) 10

56) 8

57) $9\sqrt{3}$

CHAPTER

7 Expressions and Variables

Math topics that you'll learn in this chapter:

- ☑ Simplifying Variable Expressions
- ☑ Simplifying Polynomial Expressions
- ☑ The Distributive Property
- ☑ Evaluating One Variable
- ☑ Evaluating Two Variables

57

Simplifying Variable Expressions

- In algebra, a variable is a letter used to stand for a number. The most common letters are $x, y, z, a, b, c, m,$ and n.

- An algebraic expression is an expression that contains integers, variables, and math operations such as addition, subtraction, multiplication, division, etc.

- In an expression, we can combine "like" terms. (values with same variable and same power)

Examples:

Example 1. Simplify. $(4x + 2x + 4) =$

Solution: In this expression, there are three terms: $4x$, $2x$, and 4. Two terms are "like terms": $4x$ and $2x$. Combine like terms. $4x + 2x = 6x$. Then: $(4x + 2x + 4) = 6x + 4$ (***remember you cannot combine variables and numbers.***)

Example 2. Simplify. $-2x^2 - 5x + 4x^2 - 9 =$

Solution: Combine "like" terms: $-2x^2 + 4x^2 = 2x^2$.
Then: $-2x^2 - 5x + 4x^2 - 9 = 2x^2 - 5x - 9$.

Example 3. Simplify. $(-8 + 6x^2 + 3x^2 + 9x) =$

Solution: Combine like terms. Then:
$(-8 + 6x^2 + 3x^2 + 9x) = 9x^2 + 9x - 8$

Example 4. Simplify. $-10x + 6x^2 - 3x + 9x^2 =$

Solution: Combine "like" terms: $-10x - 3x = -13x$, and $6x^2 + 9x^2 = 15x^2$
Then: $-10x + 6x^2 - 3x + 9x^2 = -13x + 15x^2$. Write in standard form (biggest powers first): $-13x + 15x^2 = 15x^2 - 13x$

bit.ly/2WFVudQ

Find more at

Simplifying Polynomial Expressions

- In mathematics, a polynomial is an expression consisting of variables and coefficients that involves only the operations of addition, subtraction, multiplication, and non–negative integer exponents of variables.

$$P(x) = a_n x^n + a_{n-1} x^{n-1} + \dots + a_2 x^2 + a_1 x + a_0$$

- Polynomials must always be simplified as much as possible. It means you must add together any like terms. (values with same variable and same power)

Examples:

Example 1. Simplify this Polynomial Expressions. $3x^2 - 6x^3 - 2x^3 + 4x^4$

Solution: Combine "like" terms: $-6x^3 - 2x^3 = -8x^3$

Then: $3x^2 - 6x^3 - 2x^3 + 4x^4 = 3x^2 - 8x^3 + 4x^4$

Now, write the expression in standard form: $3x^2 - 8x^3 + 4x^4 = 4x^4 - 8x^3 + 3x^2$

Example 2. Simplify this expression. $(-5x^2 + 2x^3) - (3x^3 - 6x^2) =$

Solution: First, multiply $(-)$ into $(3x^3 - 6x^2)$:

$(-5x^2 + 2x^3) - (3x^3 - 6x^2) = -5x^2 + 2x^3 - 3x^3 + 6x^2$

Then combine "like" terms: $-5x^2 + 2x^3 - 3x^3 + 6x^2 = x^2 - x^3$

And write in standard form: $x^2 - x^3 = -x^3 + x^2$

Example 3. Simplify. $3x^3 - 9x^4 - 8x^2 + 12x^4 =$

Solution: Combine "like" terms: $-9x^4 + 12x^4 = 3x^4$

Then: $3x^3 - 9x^4 - 8x^2 + 12x^4 = 3x^3 + 3x^4 - 8x^2$

And write in standard form: $3x^3 + 3x^4 - 8x^2 = 3x^4 + 3x^3 - 8x^2$

bit.ly/2WT5gtn
Find more at

The Distributive Property

- The distributive property (or the distributive property of multiplication over addition and subtraction) simplifies and solves expressions in the form of: $a(b + c)$ or $a(b - c)$

- The distributive property is multiplying a term outside the parentheses by the terms inside.

- Distributive Property rule: $a(b + c) = ab + ac$

Examples:

Example 1. Simply using the distributive property. $(-2)(x + 3)$

Solution: Use Distributive Property rule: $a(b + c) = ab + ac$

$(-2)(x + 3) = (-2 \times x) + (-2) \times (3) = -2x - 6$

Example 2. Simply. $(-5)(-2x - 6)$

Solution: Use Distributive Property rule: $a(b + c) = ab + ac$

$(-5)(-2x - 6) = (-5 \times -2x) + (-5) \times (-6) = 10x + 30$

Example 3. Simply. $(7)(2x - 8) - 12x$

Solution: First, simplify $(7)(2x - 8)$ using the distributive property.

Then: $(7)(2x - 8) = 14x - 56$

Now combine like terms: $(7)(2x - 8) - 12x = 14x - 56 - 12x$

In this expression, $14x$ and $-12x$ are "like terms" and we can combine them.

$14x - 12x = 2x$. Then: $14x - 56 - 12x = 2x - 56$

Evaluating One Variable

- To evaluate one variable expressions, find the variable and substitute a number for that variable.

- Perform the arithmetic operations.

Examples:

Example 1. Calculate this expression for $x = 2$. $8 + 2x$

Solution: First, substitute 2 for x.

Then: $8 + 2x = 8 + 2(2)$

Now, use order of operation to find the answer: $8 + 2(2) = 8 + 4 = 12$

Example 2. Evaluate this expression for $x = -1$. $4x - 8$

Solution: First, substitute -1 for x.

Then: $4x - 8 = 4(-1) - 8$

Now, use order of operation to find the answer: $4(-1) - 8 = -4 - 8 = -12$

Example 3. Find the value of this expression when $x = 4$. $(16 - 5x)$

Solution: First, substitute 4 for x,

Then: $16 - 5x = 16 - 5(4) = 16 - 20 = -4$

Example 4. Solve this expression for $x = -3$. $15 + 7x$

Solution: Substitute -3 for x.

Then: $15 + 7x = 15 + 7(-3) = 15 - 21 = -6$

Evaluating Two Variables

- To evaluate an algebraic expression, substitute a number for each variable.

- Perform the arithmetic operations to find the value of the expression.

Examples:

Example 1. Calculate this expression for $a = 2$ and $b = -1$. $(4a - 3b)$

Solution: First, substitute 2 for a, and -1 for b.

Then: $4a - 3b = 4(2) - 3(-1)$

Now, use order of operation to find the answer: $4(2) - 3(-1) = 8 + 3 = 11$

Example 2. Evaluate this expression for $x = -2$ and $y = 2$. $(3x + 6y)$

Solution: Substitute -2 for x, and 2 for y.

Then: $3x + 6y = 3(-2) + 6(2) = -6 + 12 = 6$

Example 3. Find the value of this expression $2(6a - 5b)$, when $a = -1$ and $b = 4$.

Solution: Substitute -1 for a, and 4 for b.

Then: $2(6a - 5b) = 2(6(-1) - 5(4)) = 2(-6 - 20) = 2(-26) = -52$

Example 4. Evaluate this expression. $-7x - 2y$, $x = 4$, $y = -3$

Solution: Substitute 4 for x, and -3 for y and simplify.

Then: $-7x - 2y = -7(4) - 2(-3) = -28 + 6 = -22$

Chapter 7: Practices

✎ Simplify each expression.

1) $(3 + 4x - 1) =$

2) $(-5 - 2x + 7) =$

3) $(12x - 5x - 4) =$

4) $(-16x + 24x - 9) =$

5) $(6x + 5 - 15x) =$

6) $2 + 5x - 8x - 6 =$

7) $5x + 10 - 3x - 22 =$

8) $-5 - 3x^2 - 6 + 4x =$

9) $-6 + 9x^2 - 3 + x =$

10) $5x^2 + 3x - 10x - 3 =$

11) $4x^2 - 2x - 6x + 5 - 8 =$

12) $3x^2 - 5x - 7x + 2 - 4 =$

13) $9x^2 - x - 5x + 3 - 9 =$

14) $2x^2 - 7x - 3x^2 + 4x + 6 =$

✎ Simplify each polynomial.

15) $5x^2 + 3x^3 - 9x^2 + 2x =$

16) $8x^4 + 2x^5 - 7x^4 + 3x^2 =$

17) $15x^3 + 11x - 5x^2 - 9x^3 =$

18) $(7x^3 - 3x^2) + (5x^2 - 13x) =$

19) $(12x^4 + 6x^3) + (x^3 - 5x^4) =$

20) $(15x^5 - 8x^3) - (4x^3 + x^2) =$

21) $(14x^4 + 7x^3) - (x^3 - 24) =$

22) $(20x^4 + 6x^3) - (-x^3 - 2x^4) =$

23) $(x^2 + 9x^3) + (-22x^2 + 6x^3) =$

24) $(4x^4 - 2x^3) + (-5x^3 - 8x^4) =$

Effortless Math Education

✎ Use the distributive property to simply each expression.

25) $2(6 + x) =$ _____

26) $5(3 - 2x) =$ _____

27) $7(1 - 5x) =$ _____

28) $(3 - 4x)7 =$ _____

29) $6(2 - 3x) =$ _____

30) $(-1)(-9 + x) =$ _____

31) $(-6)(3x - 2) =$ _____

32) $(-x + 12)(-4) =$ _____

33) $(-2)(1 - 6x) =$ _____

34) $(-5x - 3)(-8) =$ _____

✎ Evaluate each expression using the value given.

35) $x = 4 \rightarrow 10 - x =$ ____

36) $x = 6 \rightarrow x + 8 =$ ____

37) $x = 3 \rightarrow 2x - 6 =$ ____

38) $x = 2 \rightarrow 10 - 4x =$ ____

39) $x = 7 \rightarrow 8x - 3 =$ ____

40) $x = 9 \rightarrow 20 - 2x =$ ____

41) $x = 5 \rightarrow 10x - 30 =$ ___

42) $x = -6 \rightarrow 5 - x =$ ____

43) $x = -3 \rightarrow 22 - 3x =$ ____

44) $x = -7 \rightarrow 10 - 9x =$ ____

45) $x = -10 \rightarrow 40 - 3x =$ ____

46) $x = -2 \rightarrow 20x - 5 =$ ____

47) $x = -5 \rightarrow -10x - 8 =$ ___

48) $x = -4 \rightarrow -1 - 4x =$ ___

✎ Evaluate each expression using the values given.

49) $x = 2, y = 1 \rightarrow 2x + 7y =$ _____

50) $a = 3, b = 5 \rightarrow 3a - 5b =$ _____

51) $x = 6, y = 2 \rightarrow 3x - 2y + 8 =$ _____

52) $a = -2, b = 3 \rightarrow -5a + 2b + 6 =$ _____

53) $x = -4, y = -3 \rightarrow -4x + 10 - 8y =$ _____

Effortless

Math

Education

Chapter 7: Answers

1) $4x + 2$

2) $-2x + 2$

3) $7x - 4$

4) $8x - 9$

5) $-9x + 5$

6) $-3x - 4$

7) $2x - 12$

8) $-3x^2 + 4x - 11$

9) $9x^2 + x - 9$

10) $5x^2 - 7x - 3$

11) $4x^2 - 8x - 3$

12) $3x^2 - 12x - 2$

13) $9x^2 - 6x - 6$

14) $-x^2 - 3x + 6$

15) $3x^3 - 4x^2 + 2x$

16) $2x^5 + x^4 + 3x^2$

17) $6x^3 - 5x^2 + 11x$

18) $7x^3 + 2x^2 - 13x$

19) $7x^4 + 7x^3$

20) $15x^5 - 12x^3 - x^2$

21) $14x^4 + 6x^3 + 24$

22) $22x^4 + 7x^3$

23) $15x^3 - 21x^2$

24) $-4x^4 - 7x^3$

25) $2x + 12$

26) $-10x + 15$

27) $-35x + 7$

28) $-28x + 21$

29) $-18x + 12$

30) $-x + 9$

31) $-18x + 12$

32) $4x - 48$

33) $12x - 2$

34) $40x + 24$

35) 6

36) 14

37) 0

38) 2

39) 53

40) 2

41) 20

42) 11

43) 31

44) 73

45) 70

46) -45

47) 42

48) 15

49) 11

50) -16

51) 22

52) 22

53) 50

CHAPTER

8 Equations and Inequalities

Math topics that you'll learn in this chapter:

- ☑ One-Step Equations
- ☑ Multi-Step Equations
- ☑ System of Equations
- ☑ Graphing Single–Variable Inequalities
- ☑ One-Step Inequalities
- ☑ Multi-Step Inequalities

67

One–Step Equations

- The values of two expressions on both sides of an equation are equal. Example: $ax = b$. In this equation, ax is equal to b.

- Solving an equation means finding the value of the variable.

- You only need to perform one Math operation to solve the one-step equations.

- To solve a one-step equation, find the inverse (opposite) operation is being performed.

- The inverse operations are:

  ❖ Addition and subtraction

  ❖ Multiplication and division

Examples:

Example 1. Solve this equation for x. $4x = 16 \rightarrow x = ?$

Solution: Here, the operation is multiplication (variable x is multiplied by 4) and its inverse operation is division. To solve this equation, divide both sides of equation by 4: $4x = 16 \rightarrow \frac{4x}{4} = \frac{16}{4} \rightarrow x = 4$

Example 2. Solve this equation. $x + 8 = 0 \rightarrow x = ?$

Solution: In this equation, 8 is added to the variable x. The inverse operation of addition is subtraction. To solve this equation, subtract 8 from both sides of the equation: $x + 8 - 8 = 0 - 8$. Then: $x + 8 - 8 = 0 - 8 \rightarrow x = -8$

Example 3. Solve this equation for x. $x - 12 = 0$

Solution: Here, the operation is subtraction and its inverse operation is addition. To solve this equation, add 12 to both sides of the equation: $x - 12 + 12 = 0 + 12 \rightarrow x = 12$

bit.ly/37Jq0tK

Find more at

Multi–Step Equations

- To solve a multi-step equation, combine "like" terms on one side.

- Bring variables to one side by adding or subtracting.

- Simplify using the inverse of addition or subtraction.

- Simplify further by using the inverse of multiplication or division.

- Check your solution by plugging the value of the variable into the original equation.

Examples:

Example 1. Solve this equation for x. $4x + 8 = 20 - 2x$

Solution: First, bring variables to one side by adding $2x$ to both sides. Then:

$4x + 8 + 2x = 20 - 2x + 2x \rightarrow 4x + 8 + 2x = 20$.

Simplify: $6x + 8 = 20$. Now, subtract 8 from both sides of the equation:

$6x + 8 - 8 = 20 - 8 \rightarrow 6x = 12 \rightarrow$ Divide both sides by 6:

$6x = 12 \rightarrow \dfrac{6x}{6} = \dfrac{12}{6} \rightarrow x = 2$

Let's check this solution by substituting the value of 2 for x in the original equation:

$x = 2 \rightarrow 4x + 8 = 20 - 2x \rightarrow 4(2) + 8 = 20 - 2(2) \rightarrow 16 = 16$

The answer $x = 2$ is correct.

Example 2. Solve this equation for x. $-5x + 4 = 24$

Solution: Subtract 4 from both sides of the equation.

$-5x + 4 = 24 \rightarrow -5x + 4 - 4 = 24 - 4 \rightarrow -5x = 20$

Divide both sides by -5, then: $-5x = 20 \rightarrow \dfrac{-5x}{-5} = \dfrac{20}{-5} \rightarrow x = -4$

Now, check the solution:

$x = -4 \rightarrow -5x + 4 = 24 \rightarrow -5(-4) + 4 = 24 \rightarrow 24 = 24$

The answer $x = -4$ is correct.

bit.ly/3nQbSEB
Find more at

System of Equations

- A system of equations contains two equations and two variables. For example, consider the system of equations: $x - y = 1$ and $x + y = 5$

- The easiest way to solve a system of equations is using the elimination method. The elimination method uses the addition property of equality. You can add the same value to each side of an equation.

- For the first equation above, you can add $x + y$ to the left side and 5 to the right side of the first equation: $x - y + (x + y) = 1 + 5$. Now, if you simplify, you get: $x - y + (x + y) = 1 + 5 \rightarrow 2x = 6 \rightarrow x = 3$. Now, substitute 3 for the x in the first equation: $3 - y = 1$. By solving this equation, $y = 2$

Example:

What is the value of $x + y$ in this system of equations?

$$\begin{cases} 2x + 4y = 12 \\ 4x - 2y = -16 \end{cases}$$

Solution: Solving a System of Equations by Elimination:

Multiply the first equation by (-2), then add it to the second equation.

$$\begin{array}{c} -2(2x + 4y = 12) \\ 4x - 2y = -16 \end{array} \Rightarrow \begin{array}{c} -4x - 8y = -24 \\ 4x - 2y = -16 \end{array} \Rightarrow (-4x) + 4x - 8y - 2y = -24 - 16 \Rightarrow$$

$$-10y = -40 \Rightarrow y = 4$$

Plug in the value of y into one of the equations and solve for x.

$2x + 4(4) = 12 \Rightarrow 2x + 16 = 12 \Rightarrow 2x = -4 \Rightarrow x = -2$

Thus, $x + y = -2 + 4 = 2$

Graphing Single–Variable Inequalities

- An inequality compares two expressions using an inequality sign.

- Inequality signs are: "less than" <, "greater than" >, "less than or equal to" ≤, and "greater than or equal to" ≥.

- To graph a single–variable inequality, find the value of the inequality on the number line.

- For less than (<) or greater than (>) draw an open circle on the value of the variable. If there is an equal sign too, then use a filled circle.

- Draw an arrow to the right for greater or to the left for less than.

Examples:

Example 1. Draw a graph for this inequality. $x > 2$

Solution: Since the variable is greater than 2, then we need to find 2 in the number line and draw an open circle on it. Then, draw an arrow to the right.

Example 2. Graph this inequality. $x \leq -3$.

Solution: Since the variable is less than or equal to −3, then we need to find −3 on the number line and draw a filled circle on it. Then, draw an arrow to the left.

One–Step Inequalities

- An inequality compares two expressions using an inequality sign.
- Inequality signs are: "less than" <, "greater than" >, "less than or equal to" ≤, and "greater than or equal to" ≥.
- You only need to perform one Math operation to solve the one-step inequalities.
- To solve one-step inequalities, find the inverse (opposite) operation is being performed.
- For dividing or multiplying both sides by negative numbers, flip the direction of the inequality sign.

Examples:

Example 1. Solve this inequality for x. $x + 5 \geq 4$

Solution: The inverse (opposite) operation of addition is subtraction. In this inequality, 5 is added to x. To isolate x we need to subtract 5 from both sides of the inequality.

Then: $x + 5 \geq 4 \rightarrow x + 5 - 5 \geq 4 - 5 \rightarrow x \geq -1$. The solution is: $x \geq -1$

Example 2. Solve the inequality. $x - 3 > -6$

Solution: 3 is subtracted from x. Add 3 to both sides.

$x - 3 > -6 \rightarrow x - 3 + 3 > -6 + 3 \rightarrow x > -3$

Example 3. Solve. $4x \leq -8$

Solution: 4 is multiplied to x. Divide both sides by 4.

Then: $4x \leq -8 \rightarrow \frac{4x}{4} \leq \frac{-8}{4} \rightarrow x \leq -2$

Example 4. Solve. $-3x \leq 6$

Solution: -3 is multiplied to x. Divide both sides by -3. Remember when dividing or multiplying both sides of an inequality by negative numbers, flip the direction of the inequality sign.

Then: $-3x \leq 6 \rightarrow \frac{-3x}{-3} \geq \frac{6}{-3} \rightarrow x \geq -2$

Multi−Step Inequalities

- To solve a multi-step inequality, combine "like" terms on one side.

- Bring variables to one side by adding or subtracting.

- Isolate the variable.

- Simplify using the inverse of addition or subtraction.

- Simplify further by using the inverse of multiplication or division.

- For dividing or multiplying both sides by negative numbers, flip the direction of the inequality sign.

Examples:

Example 1. Solve this inequality. $8x - 2 \leq 14$

Solution: In this inequality, 2 is subtracted from $8x$. The inverse of subtraction is addition. Add 2 to both sides of the inequality:

$8x - 2 + 2 \leq 14 + 2 \rightarrow 8x \leq 16$

Now, divide both sides by 8. Then: $8x \leq 16 \rightarrow \frac{8x}{8} \leq \frac{16}{8} \rightarrow x \leq 2$

The solution of this inequality is $x \leq 2$.

Example 2. Solve this inequality. $3x + 9 < 12$

Solution: First, subtract 9 from both sides: $3x + 9 - 9 < 12 - 9$

Then simplify: $3x + 9 - 9 < 12 - 9 \rightarrow 3x < 3$

Now divide both sides by 3: $\frac{3x}{3} < \frac{3}{3} \rightarrow x < 1$

Example 3. Solve this inequality. $-5x + 3 \geq 8$

Solution: First, subtract 3 from both sides:

$-5x + 3 - 3 \geq 8 - 3 \rightarrow -5x \geq 5$

Divide both sides by -5. Remember that you need to flip the direction of inequality sign. $-5x \geq 5 \rightarrow \frac{-5x}{-5} \leq \frac{5}{-5} \rightarrow x \leq -1$

bit.ly/2WK1xOr

Find more at

Chapter 8: Practices

✎ Solve each equation. (One–Step Equations)

1) $x + 6 = 3 \rightarrow x =$ ____

2) $5 = 11 - x \rightarrow x =$ ____

3) $-3 = 8 + x \rightarrow x =$ ____

4) $x - 2 = -7 \rightarrow x =$ ____

5) $-15 = x + 6 \rightarrow x =$ ____

6) $10 - x = -2 \rightarrow x =$ ____

7) $22 - x = -9 \rightarrow x =$ ____

8) $-4 + x = 28 \rightarrow x =$ ____

9) $11 - x = -7 \rightarrow x =$ ____

10) $35 - x = -7 \rightarrow x =$ ____

✎ Solve each equation. (Multi–Step Equations)

11) $4(x + 2) = 12 \rightarrow x =$ ____

12) $-6(6 - x) = 12 \rightarrow x =$ ____

13) $5 = -5(x + 2) \rightarrow x =$ ____

14) $-10 = 2(4 + x) \rightarrow x =$ ____

15) $4(x + 2) = -12, x =$ ____

16) $-6(3 + 2x) = 30, x =$ ____

17) $-3(4 - x) = 12, x =$ ____

18) $-4(6 - x) = 16, x =$ ____

✎ Solve each system of equations.

19) $\begin{cases} x + 6y = 32 \\ x + 3y = 17 \end{cases}$ $x =$ ____ $y =$ ____

20) $\begin{cases} 3x + y = 15 \\ x + 2y = 10 \end{cases}$ $x =$ ____ $y =$ ____

21) $\begin{cases} 3x + 5y = 17 \\ 2x + y = 9 \end{cases}$ $x =$ ____ $y =$ ____

22) $\begin{cases} 5x - 2y = -8 \\ -6x + 2y = 10 \end{cases}$ $x =$ ____ $y =$ ____

Effortless

Math

Education

✏️ **Draw a graph for each inequality.**

23)$x \leq -3$

24)$x > -5$

✏️ **Solve each inequality and graph it.**

25)$x - 2 \geq -2$

26)$2x - 3 < 9$

✏️ **Solve each inequality.**

27)$x + 13 > 4$

28)$x + 6 > 5$

29)$-12 + 2x \leq 26$

30)$-2 + 8x \leq 14$

31)$6 + 4x \leq 18$

32)$4(x + 3) \geq -12$

33)$2(6 + x) \geq -12$

34)$3(x - 5) < -6$

35)$10 + 5x < -15$

36)$6(6 + x) \geq -18$

37)$2(x - 5) \geq -14$

38)$6(x + 4) < -12$

39)$3(x - 8) \geq -48$

40)$-(6 - 4x) > -30$

41)$2(2 + 2x) > -60$

42)$-3(4 + 2x) > -24$

Effortless
Math
Education

Chapter 8: Answers

1) -3

2) 6

3) -11

4) -5

5) -21

6) 12

7) 31

8) 32

9) 18

10) 42

11) 1

12) 8

13) -3

14) -9

15) -5

16) -4

17) 8

18) 10

19) $x = 2, y = 5$

20) $x = 4, y = 3$

21) $x = 4, y = 1$

22) $x = -2, y = -1$

23) $x \leq -3$

24) $x > -5$

25) $x \geq 0$

26) $x < 6$

27) $x > -9$

28) $x > -1$

29) $x \leq 19$

30) $x \leq 2$

31) $x \leq 3$

32) $x \geq -6$

33) $x \geq -12$

34) $x < 3$

35) $x < -5$

36) $x \geq -9$

37) $x \geq -2$

38) $x < -6$

39) $x \geq -8$

40) $x > -6$

41) $x > -16$

42) $x < 2$

Effortless
Math
Education

CHAPTER

9 Lines and Slope

Math topics that you'll learn in this chapter:

☑ Finding Slope

☑ Graphing Lines Using Slope–Intercept Form

☑ Writing Linear Equations

☑ Finding Midpoint

☑ Finding Distance of Two Points

☑ Graphing Linear Inequalities

77

Finding Slope

- The slope of a line represents the direction of a line on the coordinate plane.

- A coordinate plane contains two perpendicular number lines. The horizontal line is x and the vertical line is y. The point at which the two axes intersect is called the origin. An ordered pair (x, y) shows the location of a point.

- A line on a coordinate plane can be drawn by connecting two points.

- To find the slope of a line, we need the equation of the line or two points on the line.

- The slope of a line with two points A (x_1, y_1) and B (x_2, y_2) can be found by using this formula: $\frac{y_2 - y_1}{x_2 - x_1} = \frac{rise}{run}$

- The equation of a line is typically written as $y = mx + b$ where m is the slope and b is the y-intercept.

Examples:

Example 1. Find the slope of the line through these two points:

$$A(1, -6) \ and \ B(3, 2).$$

Solution: Slope $= \frac{y_2 - y_1}{x_2 - x_1}$. Let (x_1, y_1) be A$(1, -6)$ and (x_2, y_2) be $B(3, 2)$.

(Remember, you can choose any point for (x_1, y_1) and (x_2, y_2)).

Then: slope $= \frac{y_2 - y_1}{x_2 - x_1} = \frac{2 - (-6)}{3 - 1} = \frac{8}{2} = 4$

The slope of the line through these two points is 4.

Example 2. Find the slope of the line with equation $y = -2x + 8$

bit.ly/3nMJYJv

Find more at

Solution: When the equation of a line is written in the form of $y = mx + b$, the slope is m. In this line: $y = -2x + 8$, the slope is -2.

EffortlessMath.com

Graphing Lines Using Slope–Intercept Form

- Slope–intercept form of a line: given the slope **m** and the **y**–intercept (the intersection of the line and *y*-axis) **b**, then the equation of the line is:

$$y = mx + b$$

- To draw the graph of a linear equation in a slope-intercept form on the *xy* coordinate plane, find two points on the line by plugging two values for *x* and calculating the values of *y*.

- You can also use the slope (*m*) and one point to graph the line.

Example:

Sketch the graph of $y = 2x - 4$.

Solution: To graph this line, we need to find two points. When *x* is zero the value of *y* is −4. And when *x* is 2 the value of *y* is 0.

$$x = 0 \rightarrow y = 2(0) - 4 = -4,$$

$$y = 0 \rightarrow 0 = 2x - 4 \rightarrow x = 2$$

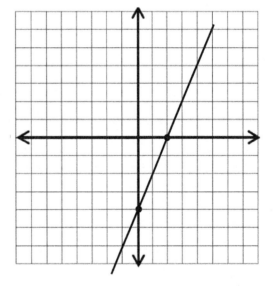

Now, we have two points:

$(0, -4)$ and $(2, 0)$.

Find the points on the coordinate plane and graph the line. Remember that the slope of the line is 2.

Writing Linear Equations

- The equation of a line in slope-intercept form: $y = mx + b$

- To write the equation of a line, first identify the slope.

- Find the y-intercept. This can be done by substituting the slope and the coordinates of a point (x, y) on the line.

Examples:

Example 1. What is the equation of the line that passes through $(3, -4)$ and has a slope of 6?

Solution: The general slope-intercept form of the equation of a line is $y = mx + b$, where m is the slope and b is the y-intercept.
By substitution of the given point and given slope:
$y = mx + b \rightarrow -4 = (6)(3) + b$. So, $b = -4 - 18 = -22$, and the required equation of the line is: $y = 6x - 22$

Example 2. Write the equation of the line through two points $A(3, 1)$ and $B(-2, 6)$.

Solution: First, find the slope: $Slop = \frac{y_2 - y_1}{x_2 - x_1} = \frac{6-1}{-2-3} = \frac{5}{-5} = -1 \rightarrow m = -1$

To find the value of b, use either points and plug in the values of x and y in the equation. The answer will be the same: $y = -x + b$. Let's check both points.
Then: $(3, 1) \rightarrow y = mx + b \rightarrow 1 = -1(3) + b \rightarrow b = 4$
$(-2, 6) \rightarrow y = mx + b \rightarrow 6 = -1(-2) + b \rightarrow b = 4$.
The y-intercept of the line is 4. The equation of the line is: $y = -x + 4$

Example 3. What is the equation of the line that passes through $(4, -1)$ and has a slope of 4?

Solution: The general slope-intercept form of the equation of a line is $y = mx + b$, where m is the slope and b is the y-intercept. By substitution of the given point and given slope: $y = mx + b \rightarrow -1 = (4)(4) + b$
So, $b = -1 - 16 = -17$, and the equation of the line is: $y = 4x - 17$.

Finding Midpoint

- The middle of a line segment is its midpoint.

- The Midpoint of two endpoints A (x_1, y_1) and B (x_2, y_2) can be found using this formula: M $(\frac{x_1+x_2}{2}, \frac{y_1+y_2}{2})$

Examples:

Example 1. Find the midpoint of the line segment with the given endpoints. $(2, -4), (6, 8)$

Solution: Midpoint $= \left(\frac{x_1+x_2}{2}, \frac{y_1+y_2}{2}\right) \to (x_1, y_1) = (2, -4)$ and $(x_2, y_2) = (6, 8)$

Midpoint $= \left(\frac{2+6}{2}, \frac{-4+8}{2}\right) \to \left(\frac{8}{2}, \frac{4}{2}\right) \to M(4, 2)$

Example 2. Find the midpoint of the line segment with the given endpoints. $(-2, 3), (6, -7)$

Solution: Midpoint $= \left(\frac{x_1+x_2}{2}, \frac{y_1+y_2}{2}\right) \to (x_1, y_1) = (-2, 3)$ and $(x_2, y_2) = (6, -7)$

Midpoint $= \left(\frac{-2+6}{2}, \frac{3+(-7)}{2}\right) \to \left(\frac{4}{2}, \frac{-4}{2}\right) \to M(2, -2)$

Example 3. Find the midpoint of the line segment with the given endpoints. $(7, -4), (1, 8)$

Solution: Midpoint $= \left(\frac{x_1+x_2}{2}, \frac{y_1+y_2}{2}\right) \to (x_1, y_1) = (7, -4)$ and $(x_2, y_2) = (1, 8)$

Midpoint $= \left(\frac{7+1}{2}, \frac{-4+8}{2}\right) \to \left(\frac{8}{2}, \frac{4}{2}\right) \to M(4, 2)$

Example 4. Find the midpoint of the line segment with the given endpoints. $(6, 3), (10, -9)$

Solution: Midpoint $= \left(\frac{x_1+x_2}{2}, \frac{y_1+y_2}{2}\right) \to (x_1, y_1) = (6, 3)$ and $(x_2, y_2) = (10, -3)$

Midpoint $= \left(\frac{6+10}{2}, \frac{3-9}{2}\right) \to \left(\frac{16}{2}, \frac{-6}{2}\right) \to M(8, -3)$

bit.ly/3nPdnTq

Find more at

Finding Distance of Two Points

- Use the following formula to find the distance of two points with the coordinates A (x_1, y_1) and B (x_2, y_2):

$$d = \sqrt{(x_2 - x_1)^2 + (y_2 - y_1)^2}$$

Examples:

Example 1. Find the distance between $(4, 2)$ and $(-5, -10)$ on the coordinate plane.

Solution: Use distance of two points formula: $d = \sqrt{(x_2 - x_1)^2 + (y_2 - y_1)^2}$

$(x_1, y_1) = (4, 2)$ and $(x_2, y_2) = (-5, -10)$. Then: $d = \sqrt{(x_2 - x_1)^2 + (y_2 - y_1)^2} \rightarrow$

$$= \sqrt{(-5 - 4)^2 + (-10 - 2)^2} = \sqrt{(-9)^2 + (-12)^2} = \sqrt{81 + 144} = \sqrt{225} = 15$$

Then: $d = 15$

Example 2. Find the distance of two points $(-1, 5)$ and $(-4, 1)$.

Solution: Use distance of two points formula: $d = \sqrt{(x_2 - x_1)^2 + (y_2 - y_1)^2}$

$(x_1, y_1) = (-1, 5)$, and $(x_2, y_2) = (-4, 1)$

Then: $= \sqrt{(x_2 - x_1)^2 + (y_2 - y_1)^2} \rightarrow d = \sqrt{(-4 - (-1))^2 + (1 - 5)^2} =$

$\sqrt{(-3)^2 + (-4)^2} = \sqrt{9 + 16} = \sqrt{25} = 5$. Then: $d = 5$

Example 3. Find the distance between $(-6, 5)$ and $(-1, -7)$.

Solution: Use distance of two points formula: $d = \sqrt{(x_2 - x_1)^2 + (y_2 - y_1)^2}$

$(x_1, y_1) = (-6, 5)$ and $(x_2, y_2) = (-1, -7)$. Then: $d = \sqrt{(x_2 - x_1)^2 + (y_2 - y_1)^2}$

$$d = \sqrt{\left(-1 - (-6)\right)^2 + (-7 - 5)^2} = \sqrt{(5)^2 + (-12)^2} = \sqrt{25 + 144} = \sqrt{169}$$

$$= 13$$

Graphing Linear Inequalities

- To graph a linear inequality, first draw a graph of the "equals" line.

- Use a dash line for less than (<) and greater than (>) signs and a solid line for less than and equal to (≤) and greater than and equal to (≥).

- Choose a testing point. (it can be any point on both sides of the line.)

- Put the value of (x, y) of that point in the inequality. If that works, that part of the line is the solution. If the values don't work, then the other part of the line is the solution.

Example:

Sketch the graph of inequality: $y < 2x + 4$

Solution: To draw the graph of $y < 2x + 4$, you first need to graph the line:

$y = 2x + 4$

Since there is a less than (<) sign, draw a dash line.

The slope is 2 and y-intercept is 4.

Then, choose a testing point and substitute the value of x and y from that point into the inequality. The easiest point to test is the origin: $(0,0)$

$$(0,0) \rightarrow y < 2x + 4 \rightarrow 0 < 2(0) + 4 \rightarrow 0 < 4$$

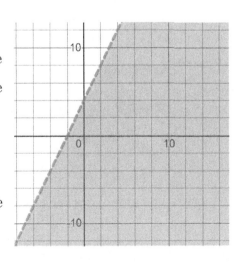

This is correct! 0 is less than 4. So, this part of the line (on the right side) is the solution of this inequality.

Chapter 9: Practices

✍ Find the slope of each line.

1) $y = x - 5$

2) $y = 2x + 6$

3) $y = -5x - 8$

4) Line through $(2, 6)$ *and* $(5, 0)$

5) Line through $(8, 0)$ *and* $(-4, 3)$

6) Line through $(-2, -4)$ *and* $(-4, 8)$

✍ Sketch the graph of each line. (Using Slope−Intercept Form)

7) $y = x + 4$

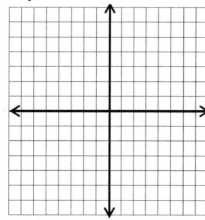

8) $y = 2x - 5$

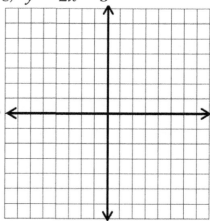

✍ Solve.

9) What is the equation of a line with slope 4 and intercept 16? _____

10) What is the equation of a line with slope 3 and passes through point $(1, 5)$?

_____

11) What is the equation of a line with slope -5 and passes through point $(-2, 7)$?

_____

12) The slope of a line is -4 and it passes through point $(-6, 2)$. What is the equation of the line? _____

13) The slope of a line is -3 and it passes through point $(-3, -6)$. What is the equation of the line? _____

✎ **Sketch the graph of each linear inequality.**

14) $y > 2x - 2$

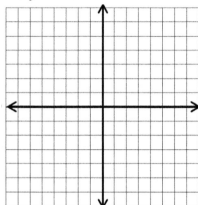

15) $y < -x + 3$

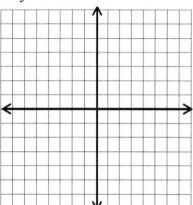

✎ **Find the midpoint of the line segment with the given endpoints.**

16) $(5, 0), (1, 4)$

17) $(2, 3), (4, 7)$

18) $(8, 1), (2, 5)$

19) $(5, 10), (3, 6)$

20) $(4, -1), (-2, 7)$

21) $(2, -5), (4, 1)$

22) $(7, 6), (-5, 2)$

23) $(-2, 8), (4, -6)$

✎ **Find the distance between each pair of points.**

24) $(-2, 8), (-6, 8)$

25) $(4, -4), (14, 20)$

26) $(-1, 9), (-5, 6)$

27) $(0, 3), (4, 3)$

28) $(0, -2), (5, 10)$

29) $(4, 3), (7, -1)$

30) $(2, 6), (10, -9)$

31) $(3, 3), (6, -1)$

32) $(-2, -12), (14, 18)$

33) $(2, -2), (12, 22)$

Effortless
Math
Education

Chapter 9: Answers

1) 1

3) -5

5) $-\dfrac{1}{4}$

2) 2

4) -2

6) -6

7) $y = x + 4$

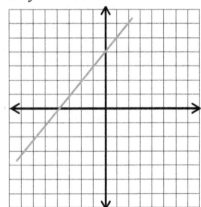

8) $y = 2x - 5$

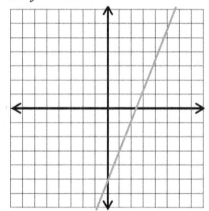

9) $y = 4x + 16$

11) $y = -5x - 3$

13) $y = -3x - 15$

10) $y = 3x + 2$

12) $y = -4x - 22$

14) $y > 2x - 2$

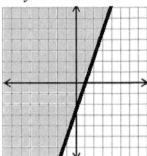

15) $y < -x + 3$

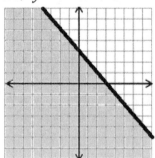

16) $(3, 2)$

20) $(1, 3)$

27) 4

17) $(3, 5)$

21) $(3, -2)$

28) 13

18) $(5, 3)$

22) $(1, 4)$

29) 5

19) $(4, 8)$

23) $(1, 1)$

30) 17

24) 4

31) 5

25) 26

32) 34

26) 5

33) 26

CHAPTER

10 Polynomials

Math topics that you'll learn in this chapter:

- ☑ Simplifying Polynomials
- ☑ Adding and Subtracting Polynomials
- ☑ Multiplying Monomials
- ☑ Multiplying and Dividing Monomials
- ☑ Multiplying a Polynomial and a Monomial
- ☑ Multiplying Binomials
- ☑ Factoring Trinomials

Simplifying Polynomials

- To simplify Polynomials, find "like" terms. (they have same variables with same power).

- Use "FOIL". (First–Out–In–Last) for binomials:

$$(x + a)(x + b) = x^2 + (b + a)x + ab$$

- Add or Subtract "like" terms using order of operation.

Examples:

Example 1. Simplify this expression. $x(4x + 7) - 2x =$

Solution: Use Distributive Property: $x(4x + 7) = 4x^2 + 7x$

Now, combine like terms: $x(4x + 7) - 2x = 4x^2 + 7x - 2x = 4x^2 + 5x$

Example 2. Simplify this expression. $(x + 3)(x + 5) =$

Solution: First, apply the FOIL method: $(a + b)(c + d) = ac + ad + bc + bd$

$(x + 3)(x + 5) = x^2 + 5x + 3x + 15$

Now combine like terms: $x^2 + 5x + 3x + 15 = x^2 + 8x + 15$

Example 3. Simplify this expression. $2x(x - 5) - 3x^2 + 6x =$

Solution: Use Distributive Property: $2x(x - 5) = 2x^2 - 10x$

Then: $2x(x - 5) - 3x^2 + 6x = 2x^2 - 10x - 3x^2 + 6x$

Now combine like terms: $2x^2 - 3x^2 = -x^2$, and $-10x + 6x = -4x$

The simplified form of the expression: $2x^2 - 10x - 3x^2 + 6 = -x^2 - 4x$

Adding and Subtracting Polynomials

- Adding polynomials is just a matter of combining like terms, with some order of operations considerations thrown in.

- Be careful with the minus signs, and don't confuse addition and multiplication!

- For subtracting polynomials, sometimes you need to use the Distributive Property: $a(b + c) = ab + ac$, $a(b - c) = ab - ac$

Examples:

Example 1. Simplify the expressions. $(x^2 - 2x^3) - (x^3 - 3x^2) =$

Solution: First, use Distributive Property:
$-(x^3 - 3x^2) = -x^3 + 3x^2$
$\rightarrow (x^2 - 2x^3) - (x^3 - 3x^2) = x^2 - 2x^3 - x^3 + 3x^2$
Now combine like terms: $-2x^3 - x^3 = -3x^3$ and $x^2 + 3x^2 = 4x^2$
Then: $(x^2 - 2x^3) - (x^3 - 3x^2) = x^2 - 2x^3 - x^3 + 3x^2 = -3x^3 + 4x^2$

Example 2. Add expressions. $(3x^3 - 5) + (4x^3 - 2x^2) =$

Solution: Remove parentheses:
$$(3x^3 - 5) + (4x^3 - 2x^2) = 3x^3 - 5 + 4x^3 - 2x^2$$
Now combine like terms: $3x^3 - 5 + 4x^3 - 2x^2 = 7x^3 - 2x^2 - 5$

Example 3. Simplify the expressions. $(-4x^2 - 2x^3) - (5x^2 + 2x^3) =$

Solution: First, use Distributive Property: $-(5x^2 + 2x^3) = -5x^2 - 2x^3 \rightarrow$
$$(-4x^2 - 2x^3) - (5x^2 + 2x^3) = -4x^2 - 2x^3 - 5x^2 - 2x^3$$
Now combine like terms and write in standard form:
$-4x^2 - 2x^3 - 5x^2 - 2x^3 = -4x^3 - 9x^2$

bit.ly/2KUgHqQ

Find more at

Multiplying Monomials

-   A monomial is a polynomial with just one term: Examples: $2x$ or $7y^2$.

-   When you multiply monomials, first multiply the coefficients (a number placed before and multiplying the variable) and then multiply the variables using multiplication property of exponents.

$$x^a \times x^b = x^{a+b}$$

Examples:

Example 1. Multiply expressions. $2xy^3 \times 6x^4y^2$

Solution: Find the same variables and use multiplication property of exponents: $x^a \times x^b = x^{a+b}$
$x \times x^4 = x^{1+4} = x^5$ and $y^3 \times y^2 = y^{3+2} = y^5$
Then, multiply coefficients and variables: $2xy^3 \times 6x^4y^2 = 12x^5y^5$

Example 2. Multiply expressions. $7a^3b^8 \times 3a^6b^4 =$

Solution: Use the multiplication property of exponents: $x^a \times x^b = x^{a+b}$
$a^3 \times a^6 = a^{3+6} = a^9$ and $b^8 \times b^4 = b^{8+4} = b^{12}$
Then: $7a^3b^8 \times 3a^6b^4 = 21a^9b^{12}$

Example 3. Multiply. $5x^2y^4z^3 \times 4x^4y^7z^5$

Solution: Use the multiplication property of exponents: $x^a \times x^b = x^{a+b}$
$x^2 \times x^4 = x^{2+4} = x^6$, $y^4 \times y^7 = y^{4+7} = y^{11}$ and $z^3 \times z^5 = z^{3+5} = z^8$
Then: $5x^2y^4z^3 \times 4x^4y^7z^5 = 20x^6y^{11}z^8$

Example 4. Simplify. $(-6a^7b^4)(4a^8b^5) =$

Solution: Use the multiplication property of exponents: $x^a \times x^b = x^{a+b}$
$a^7 \times a^8 = a^{7+8} = a^{15}$ and $b^4 \times b^5 = b^{4+5} = b^9$
Then: $(-6a^7b^4)(4a^8b^5) = -24a^{15}b^9$

Multiplying and Dividing Monomials

- When you divide or multiply two monomials, you need to divide or multiply their coefficients and then divide or multiply their variables.

- In case of exponents with the same base, for Division, subtract their powers, for Multiplication, add their powers.

- Exponent's Multiplication and Division rules:

$$x^a \times x^b = x^{a+b}, \qquad \frac{x^a}{x^b} = x^{a-b}$$

Examples:

Example 1. Multiply expressions. $(3x^5)(9x^4) =$

Solution: Use multiplication property of exponents:

$x^a \times x^b = x^{a+b} \rightarrow x^5 \times x^4 = x^9$

Then: $(3x^5)(9x^4) = 27x^9$

Example 2. Divide expressions. $\frac{12x^4y^6}{6xy^2} =$

Solution: Use division property of exponents:

$\frac{x^a}{x^b} = x^{a-b} \rightarrow \frac{x^4}{x} = x^{4-1} = x^3$ and $\frac{y^6}{y^2} = y^{6-2} = y^4$

Then: $\frac{12x^4y^6}{6xy^2} = 2x^3y^4$

Example 3. Divide expressions. $\frac{49a^6b^9}{7a^3b^4}$

Solution: Use division property of exponents:

$\frac{x^a}{x^b} = x^{a-b} \rightarrow \frac{a^6}{a^3} = a^{6-3} = a^3$ and $\frac{b^9}{b^4} = b^{9-4} = b^5$

Then: $\frac{49a^6b^9}{7a^3b^4} = 7a^3b^5$

Multiplying a Polynomial and a Monomial

- When multiplying monomials, use the product rule for exponents.

$$x^a \times x^b = x^{a+b}$$

- When multiplying a monomial by a polynomial, use the distributive property.

$$a \times (b + c) = a \times b + a \times c = ab + ac$$
$$a \times (b - c) = a \times b - a \times c = ab - ac$$

Examples:

Example 1. Multiply expressions. $6x(2x + 5)$

Solution: Use Distributive Property:

$6x(2x + 5) = 6x \times 2x + 6x \times 5 = 12x^2 + 30x$

Example 2. Multiply expressions. $x(3x^2 + 4y^2)$

Solution: Use Distributive Property:

$x(3x^2 + 4y^2) = x \times 3x^2 + x \times 4y^2 = 3x^3 + 4xy^2$

Example 3. Multiply. $-x(-2x^2 + 4x + 5)$

Solution: Use Distributive Property:

$-x(-2x^2 + 4x + 5) = (-x)(-2x^2) + (-x) \times (4x) + (-x) \times (5) =$

Now simplify:

$(-x)(-2x^2) + (-x) \times (4x) + (-x) \times (5) = 2x^3 - 4x^2 - 5x$

Multiplying Binomials

- A binomial is a polynomial that is the sum or the difference of two terms, each of which is a monomial.

- To multiply two binomials, use the "FOIL" method. (First–Out–In–Last)

$$(x + a)(x + b) = x \times x + x \times b + a \times x + a \times b = x^2 + bx + ax + ab$$

Examples:

Example 1. Multiply Binomials. $(x + 3)(x - 2) =$

Solution: Use "FOIL". (First–Out–In–Last):
$(x + 3)(x - 2) = x^2 - 2x + 3x - 6$
Then combine like terms: $x^2 - 2x + 3x - 6 = x^2 + x - 6$

Example 2. Multiply. $(x + 6)(x + 4) =$

Solution: Use "FOIL". (First–Out–In–Last):
$(x + 6)(x + 4) = x^2 + 4x + 6x + 24$
Then simplify: $x^2 + 4x + 6x + 24 = x^2 + 10x + 24$

Example 3. Multiply. $(x + 5)(x - 7) =$

Solution: Use "FOIL". (First–Out–In–Last):
$(x + 5)(x - 7) = x^2 - 7x + 5x - 35$
Then simplify: $x^2 - 7x + 5x - 35 = x^2 - 2x - 35$

Example 4. Multiply Binomials. $(x - 9)(x - 5) =$

Solution: Use "FOIL". (First–Out–In–Last):
$(x - 9)(x - 5) = x^2 - 5x - 9x + 45$
Then combine like terms: $x^2 - 5x - 9x + 45 = x^2 - 14x + 45$

bit.ly/3aCsOFL

Find more at

Factoring Trinomials

To factor trinomials, you can use following methods:

- "FOIL": $(x + a)(x + b) = x^2 + (b + a)x + ab$

- "Difference of Squares":

$$a^2 - b^2 = (a + b)(a - b)$$
$$a^2 + 2ab + b^2 = (a + b)(a + b)$$
$$a^2 - 2ab + b^2 = (a - b)(a - b)$$

- "Reverse FOIL": $x^2 + (b + a)x + ab = (x + a)(x + b)$

Examples:

Example 1. Factor this trinomial. $x^2 - 2x - 8$

Solution: Break the expression into groups. You need to find two numbers that their product is -8 and their sum is -2. (remember "Reverse FOIL": $x^2 + (b + a)x + ab = (x + a)(x + b)$). Those two numbers are 2 and -4. Then:

$$x^2 - 2x - 8 = (x^2 + 2x) + (-4x - 8)$$

Now factor out x from $x^2 + 2x : x(x + 2)$, and factor out -4 from

$-4x - 8: -4(x + 2)$; Then: $(x^2 + 2x) + (-4x - 8) = x(x + 2) - 4(x + 2)$

Now factor out like term: $(x + 2)$. Then: $(x + 2)(x - 4)$

Example 2. Factor this trinomial. $x^2 - 2x - 24$

Solution: Break the expression into groups: $(x^2 + 4x) + (-6x - 24)$

Now factor out x from $x^2 + 4x : x(x + 4)$, and factor out -6 from

$-6x - 24: -6(x + 4)$; Then: $(x + 4) - 6(x + 4)$, now factor out like term:

$(x = 4) \rightarrow x(x + 4) - 6(x + 4) = (x + 4)(x - 6)$

Chapter 10: Practices

✍ Simplify each polynomial.

1) $3(6x + 4) =$

2) $5(3x - 8) =$

3) $x(7x + 2) + 9x =$

4) $6x(x + 3) + 5x =$

5) $6x(3x + 1) - 5x =$

6) $x(3x - 4) + 3x^2 - 6 =$

7) $x^2 - 5 - 3x(x + 8) =$

8) $2x^2 + 7 - 6x(2x + 5) =$

✍ Add or subtract polynomials.

9) $(x^2 + 3) + (2x^2 - 4) =$

10) $(3x^2 - 6x) - (x^2 + 8x) =$

11) $(4x^3 - 3x^2) + (2x^3 - 5x^2) =$

12) $(6x^3 - 7x) - (5x^3 - 3x) =$

13) $(10x^3 + 4x^2) + (14x^2 - 8) =$

14) $(4x^3 - 9) - (3x^3 - 7x^2) =$

15) $(9x^3 + 3x) - (6x^3 - 4x) =$

16) $(7x^3 - 5x) - (3x^3 + 5x) =$

✍ Find the products. (Multiplying Monomials)

17) $3x^2 \times 8x^3 =$

18) $2x^4 \times 9x^3 =$

19) $-4a^4b \times 2ab^3 =$

20) $(-7x^3yz) \times (3xy^2z^4) =$

21) $-2a^5bc \times 6a^2b^4 =$

22) $9u^3t^2 \times (-2ut) =$

23) $12x^2z \times 3xy^3 =$

24) $11x^3z \times 5xy^5 =$

25) $-6a^3bc \times 5a^4b^3 =$

26) $-4x^6y^2 \times (-12xy) =$

Effortless
Math
Education

✎ **Simplify each expression. (Multiplying and Dividing Monomials)**

27) $(7x^2y^3)(3x^4y^2) =$

28) $(6x^3y^2)(4x^4y^3) =$

29) $(10x^8y^5)(3x^5y^7) =$

30) $(15a^3b^2)(2a^3b^8) =$

31) $\dfrac{42x^4y^2}{6x^3y} =$

32) $\dfrac{49x^5y^6}{7x^2y} =$

33) $\dfrac{63x^{15}y^{10}}{9x^8y^6} =$

34) $\dfrac{35x^8y^{12}}{5x^4y^8} =$

✎ **Find each product. (Multiplying a Polynomial and a Monomial)**

35) $3x(5x - y) =$

36) $2x(4x + y) =$

37) $7x(x - 3y) =$

38) $x(2x^2 + 2x - 4) =$

39) $5x(3x^2 + 8x + 2) =$

40) $7x(2x^2 - 9x - 5) =$

✎ **Find each product. (Multiplying Binomials)**

41) $(x - 3)(x + 3) =$

42) $(x - 6)(x + 6) =$

43) $(x + 10)(x + 4) =$

44) $(x - 6)(x + 7) =$

45) $(x + 2)(x - 5) =$

46) $(x - 10)(x + 3) =$

✎ **Factor each trinomial.**

47) $x^2 + 6x + 8 =$

48) $x^2 + 3x - 10 =$

49) $x^2 + 2x - 48 =$

50) $x^2 - 10x + 16 =$

51) $2x^2 - 10x + 12 =$

52) $3x^2 - 10x + 3 =$

Effortless

Math

Education

Chapter 10: Answers

1) $18x + 12$

2) $15x - 40$

3) $7x^2 + 11x$

4) $6x^2 + 23x$

5) $18x^2 + x$

6) $6x^2 - 4x - 6$

7) $-2x^2 - 24x - 5$

8) $-10x^2 - 30x + 7$

9) $3x^2 - 1$

10) $2x^2 - 14x$

11) $6x^3 - 8x^2$

12) $x^3 - 4x$

13) $10x^3 + 18x^2 - 8$

14) $x^3 + 7x^2 - 9$

15) $3x^3 + 7x$

16) $4x^3 - 10x$

17) $24x^5$

18) $18x^7$

19) $-8a^5b^4$

20) $-21x^4y^3z^5$

21) $-12a^7b^5c$

22) $-18u^4t^3$

23) $36x^3y^3z$

24) $55x^4y^5z$

25) $-30a^7b^4c$

26) $48x^7y^3$

27) $21x^6y^5$

28) $24x^7y^5$

29) $30x^{13}y^{12}$

30) $30a^6b^{10}$

31) $7xy$

32) $7x^3y^5$

33) $7x^7y^4$

34) $7x^4y^4$

35) $15x^2 - 3xy$

36) $8x^2 + 2xy$

37) $7x^2 - 21xy$

38) $2x^3 + 2x^2 - 4x$

39) $15x^3 + 40x^2 + 10x$

40) $14x^3 - 63x^2 - 35x$

41) $x^2 - 9$

42) $x^2 - 36$

43) $x^2 + 14x + 40$

44) $x^2 + x - 42$

45) $x^2 - 3x - 10$

46) $x^2 - 7x - 30$

47) $(x + 4)(x + 2)$

48) $(x + 5)(x - 2)$

49) $(x - 6)(x + 8)$

50) $(x - 8)(x - 2)$

51) $(2x - 4)(x - 3)$

52) $(3x - 1)(x - 3)$

CHAPTER 11

Geometry and Solid Figures

Math topics that you'll learn in this chapter:

- ☑ The Pythagorean Theorem
- ☑ Complementary and Supplementary angles
- ☑ Parallel lines and Transversals
- ☑ Triangles
- ☑ Special Right Triangles
- ☑ Polygons
- ☑ Circles
- ☑ Trapezoids
- ☑ Cubes
- ☑ Rectangle Prisms
- ☑ Cylinder

The Pythagorean Theorem

- You can use the Pythagorean Theorem to find a missing side in a right triangle.

- In any right triangle: $a^2 + b^2 = c^2$

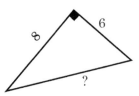

Examples:

Example 1. Right triangle ABC (not shown) has two legs of lengths 3 cm (AB) and 4 cm (AC). What is the length of the hypotenuse of the triangle (side BC)?

Solution: Use Pythagorean Theorem: $a^2 + b^2 = c^2$, $a = 3$, and $b = 4$

Then: $a^2 + b^2 = c^2 \rightarrow 3^2 + 4^2 = c^2 \rightarrow 9 + 16 = c^2 \rightarrow 25 = c^2 \rightarrow c = \sqrt{25} = 5$

The length of the hypotenuse is 5 cm.

Example 2. Find the hypotenuse of this triangle.

Solution: Use Pythagorean Theorem: $a^2 + b^2 = c^2$

Then: $a^2 + b^2 = c^2 \rightarrow 8^2 + 6^2 = c^2 \rightarrow 64 + 36 = c^2$

$c^2 = 100 \rightarrow c = \sqrt{100} = 10$

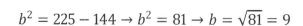

Example 3. Find the length of the missing side in this triangle.

Solution: Use Pythagorean Theorem: $a^2 + b^2 = c^2$

Then: $a^2 + b^2 = c^2 \rightarrow 12^2 + b^2 = 15^2 \rightarrow 144 + b^2 = 225 \rightarrow$

$$b^2 = 225 - 144 \rightarrow b^2 = 81 \rightarrow b = \sqrt{81} = 9$$

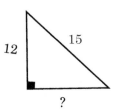

Complementary and Supplementary angles

- Two angles with a sum of 90 degrees are called complementary angles.

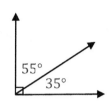

- Two angles with a sum of 180 degrees are Supplementary angles.

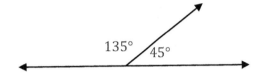

Examples:

Example 1. Find the missing angle.

Solution: Notice that the two angles form a right angle. This means that the angles are complementary, and their sum is 90. Then: $18 + x = 90 \rightarrow x = 90° - 18° = 72°$
The missing angle is 72 degrees. $x = 72°$

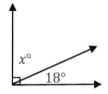

Example 2. Angles Q and S are supplementary. What is the measure of angle Q if angle S is 35 degrees?

Solution: Q and S are supplementary $\rightarrow Q + S = 180 \rightarrow Q + 35 = 180 \rightarrow$
$$Q = 180 - 35 = 145$$

Example 3. Angles x and y are complementary. What is the measure of angle x if angle y is 16 degrees?

Solution: Angles x and y are complementary $\rightarrow x + y = 90 \rightarrow x + 16 = 90 \rightarrow$
$$x = 90 - 16 = 74$$

Parallel lines and Transversals

- When a line (transversal) intersects two parallel lines in the same plane, eight angles are formed. In the following diagram, a transversal intersects two parallel lines. Angles 1, 3, 5, and 7 are congruent. Angles 2, 4, 6, and 8 are also congruent.

- In the following diagram, the following angles are supplementary angles (their sum is 180):

  ❖ Angles 1 and 8

  ❖ Angles 2 and 7

  ❖ Angles 3 and 6

  ❖ Angles 4 and 5

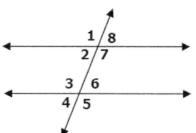

Example:

In the following diagram, two parallel lines are cut by a transversal. What is the value of x?

Solution: The two angles $3x - 15$ and $2x + 7$ are equivalent.

That is: $3x - 15 = 2x + 7$

Now, solve for x:

$3x - 15 + 15 = 2x + 7 + 15$

$\rightarrow 3x = 2x + 22 \rightarrow 3x - 2x = 2x + 22 - 2x \rightarrow$

$x = 22$

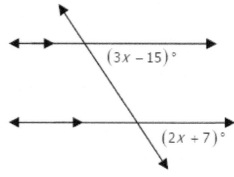

Triangles

- In any triangle, the sum of all angles is 180 degrees.
- Area of a triangle $= \frac{1}{2}(base \times height)$

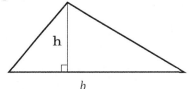

Examples:

Example 1. What is the area of this triangles?

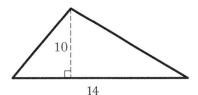

Solution: Use the area formula:
Area $= \frac{1}{2}(base \times height)$
$base = 14$ and $height = 10$, Then:
Area $= \frac{1}{2}(14 \times 10) = \frac{1}{2}(140) = 70$

Example 2. What is the area of this triangles?

Solution: Use the area formula:

Area $= \frac{1}{2}(base \times height)$
$base = 16$ and $height = 8$; Area $= \frac{1}{2}(16 \times 8) = \frac{128}{2} = 64$

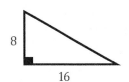

Example 3. What is the missing angle in this triangle?

Solution:

In any triangle, the sum of all angles is 180 degrees.
Let x be the missing angle.
Then: $55 + 80 + x = 180 \rightarrow 135 + x = 180 \rightarrow$
$\qquad x = 180 - 135 = 45$
The missing angle is 45 degrees.

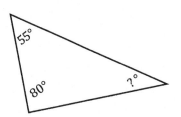

Special Right Triangles

- A special right triangle is a triangle whose sides are in a particular ratio. Two special right triangles are $45° - 45° - 90°$ and $30° - 60° - 90°$ triangles.

- In a special $45° - 45° - 90°$ triangle, the three angles are $45°$, $45°$ and $90°$. The lengths of the sides of this triangle are in the ratio of $1:1:\sqrt{2}$.

- In a special triangle $30° - 60° - 90°$, the three angles are $30° - 60° - 90°$. The lengths of this triangle are in the ratio of $1:\sqrt{3}:2$.

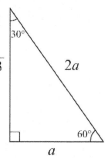

Examples:

Example 1. Find the length of the hypotenuse of a right triangle if the length of the other two sides are both 4 inches.

Solution: this is a right triangle with two equal sides. Therefore, it must be a $45° - 45° - 90°$ triangle. Two equivalent sides are 4 inches. The ratio of sides: $x: x: x\sqrt{2}$

The length of the hypotenuse is $4\sqrt{2}$ inches. $x: x: x\sqrt{2} \rightarrow 4: 4: 4\sqrt{2}$

Example 2. The length of the hypotenuse of a right triangle is 6 inches. What are the lengths of the other two sides if one angle of the triangle is $30°$?

Solution: The hypotenuse is 6 inches and the triangle is a $30° - 60° - 90°$ triangle. Then, one side of the triangle is 3 (it's half the side of the hypotenuse) and the other side is $3\sqrt{3}$. (it's the smallest side times $\sqrt{3}$)

$$x: x\sqrt{3}: 2x \rightarrow x = 3 \rightarrow x: x\sqrt{3}: 2x = 3: 3\sqrt{3}: 6$$

Polygons

- The perimeter of a square = $4 \times side = 4s$

- The perimeter of a rectangle = $2(width + length)$

- The perimeter of trapezoid = $a + b + c + d$

- The perimeter of a regular hexagon = $6a$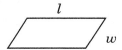

- The perimeter of a parallelogram = $2(l + w)$

Examples:

Example 1. Find the perimeter of following regular hexagon.

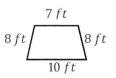

Solution: Since the hexagon is regular, all sides are equal.

Then, the perimeter of the hexagon = $6 \times (one\ side)$

The perimeter of the hexagon = $6 \times (one\ side) = 6 \times 8 = 48\ m$

Example 2. Find the perimeter of following trapezoid.

Solution: The perimeter of a trapezoid = $a + b + c + d$

The perimeter of the trapezoid = $7 + 8 + 8 + 10 = 33\ ft$

Circles

- In a circle, variable r is usually used for the radius and d for diameter.

- *Area of a circle* $= \pi r^2$ (π is about 3.14)

- *Circumference of a circle* $= 2\pi r$

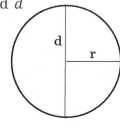

Examples:

Example 1. Find the area of this circle. ($\pi = 3.14$)

Solution:
Use area formula: $Area = \pi r^2$
$r = 6\,in \rightarrow Area = \pi(6)^2 = 36\pi$, $\pi = 3.14$
Then: $Area = 36 \times 3.14 = 113.04\,in^2$

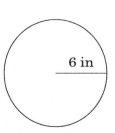

6 in

Example 2. Find the Circumference of this circle. ($\pi = 3.14$)

Solution:
Use Circumference formula: $Circumference = 2\pi r$
$r = 8\,cm \rightarrow Circumference = 2\pi(8) = 16\pi$
$\pi = 3.14$, Then: $Circumference = 16 \times 3.14 = 50.24\,cm$

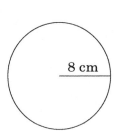

8 cm

Example 3. Find the area of this circle.

Solution:
Use area formula: $Area = \pi r^2$
$r = 9\,in$, Then: $Area = \pi(9)^2 = 25\pi$, $\pi = 3.14$
$\qquad\qquad Area = 81 \times 3.14 = 254.34\,in^2$

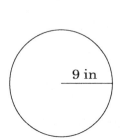

9 in

Trapezoids

- A quadrilateral with at least one pair of parallel sides is a trapezoid.

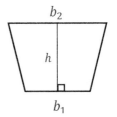

- Area of a trapezoid $= \frac{1}{2}h(b_1 + b_2)$

Examples:

Example 1. Calculate the area of this trapezoid.

Solution:

Use area formula: $A = \frac{1}{2}h(b_1 + b_2)$

$b_1 = 6\ cm$, $b_2 = 10\ cm$ and $h = 12\ cm$

Then: $A = \frac{1}{2}(12)(10 + 6) = 6(16) = 96\ cm^2$

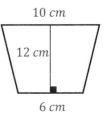

Example 2. Calculate the area of this trapezoid.

Solution:

Use area formula: $A = \frac{1}{2}h(b_1 + b_2)$

$b_1 = 10\ cm$, $b_2 = 18\ cm$ and $h = 14\ cm$

Then: $A = \frac{1}{2}(14)(10 + 18) = 196\ cm^2$

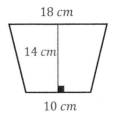

Find more at
bit.ly/3hpKACJ

Cubes

- A cube is a three-dimensional solid object bounded by six square sides.

- Volume is the measure of the amount of space inside of a solid figure, like a cube, ball, cylinder or pyramid.

- The volume of a cube = $(one\ side)^3$

- The surface area of a cube = $6 \times (one\ side)^2$

Examples:

Example 1. Find the volume and surface area of this cube.

Solution: Use volume formula: $volume = (one\ side)^3$
Then: $volume = (one\ side)^3 = (3)^3 = 27\ cm^3$
Use surface area formula:
$surface\ area\ of\ a\ cube$: $6(one\ side)^2 = 6(3)^2 = 6(9) = 54\ cm^2$

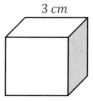
3 cm

Example 2. Find the volume and surface area of this cube.

Solution: Use volume formula: $volume = (one\ side)^3$
Then: $volume = (one\ side)^3 = (6)^3 = 216\ cm^3$
Use surface area formula:
$surface\ area\ of\ a\ cube$: $6(one\ side)^2 = 6(6)^2 = 6(36) = 216\ cm^2$

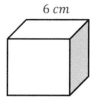
6 cm

Example 3. Find the volume and surface area of this cube.

Solution: Use volume formula: $volume = (one\ side)^3$
Then: $volume = (one\ side)^3 = (8)^3 = 512\ m^3$
Use surface area formula:
$surface\ area\ of\ a\ cube$: $6(one\ side)^2 = 6(8)^2 = 6(64) = 384\ m^2$

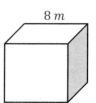
8 m

Rectangular Prisms

- A rectangular prism is a solid 3-dimensional object with six rectangular faces.

- The volume of a Rectangular prism = $Length \times Width \times Height$

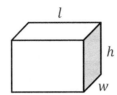

$Volume = l \times w \times h$

$Surface\ area = 2 \times (wh + lw + lh)$

Examples:

Example 1. Find the volume and surface area of this rectangular prism.

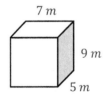

Solution: Use volume formula: $Volume = l \times w \times h$

Then: $Volume = 7 \times 5 \times 9 = 315\ m^3$

Use surface area formula: $Surface\ area = 2 \times (wh + lw + lh)$

Then: $Surface\ area = 2 \times \big((5 \times 9) + (7 \times 5) + (7 \times 9)\big)$

$$= 2 \times (45 + 35 + 63) = 2 \times (143) = 286\ m^2$$

Example 2. Find the volume and surface area of this rectangular prism.

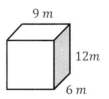

Solution: Use volume formula: $Volume = l \times w \times h$

Then: $Volume = 9 \times 6 \times 12 = 648\ m^3$

Use surface area formula: $Surface\ area = 2 \times (wh + lw + lh)$

Then: $Surface\ area = 2 \times \big((6 \times 12) + (9 \times 6) + (9 \times 12)\big)$

$$= 2 \times (72 + 54 + 108) = 2 \times (234) = 468\ m^2$$

Cylinder

- A cylinder is a solid geometric figure with straight parallel sides and a circular or oval cross-section.

- *Volume of a Cylinder = $\pi(radius)^2 \times height$, $\pi \approx 3.14$*

- *Surface area of a cylinder = $2\pi r^2 + 2\pi rh$*

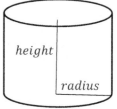

Examples:

Example 1. Find the volume and Surface area of the follow Cylinder.

Solution: Use volume formula:

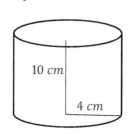

$Volume = \pi(radius)^2 \times height$

Then: $Volume = \pi(4)^2 \times 10 = 16\pi \times 10 = 160\pi$

$\pi = 3.14$, then: $Volume = 160\pi = 160 \times 3.14 = 502.4 \; cm^3$

Use surface area formula: $Surface\; area = 2\pi r^2 + 2\pi rh$

Then: $2\pi(4)^2 + 2\pi(4)(10) = 2\pi(16) + 2\pi(40) = 32\pi + 80\pi = 112\pi$

$\pi = 3.14$, Then: $Surface\; area = 112 \times 3.14 = 351.68 \; cm^2$

Example 2. Find the volume and Surface area of the follow Cylinder.

Solution: Use volume formula:

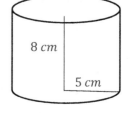

$Volume = \pi(radius)^2 \times height$

Then: $Volume = \pi(5)^2 \times 8 = 25\,\pi \times 8 = 200\pi$

$\pi = 3.14$, Then: $Volume = 200\pi = 628 \; cm^3$

Use surface area formula: $Surface\; area = 2\pi r^2 + 2\pi rh$

Then: $= 2\pi(5)^2 + 2\pi(5)(8) = 2\pi(25) + 2\pi(40) = 50\pi + 80\pi = 130\pi$

$\pi = 3.14$ then: $Surface\; area = 130 \times 3.14 = 408.2 \; cm^2$

Chapter 11: Practices

✎ Find the missing side?

1)
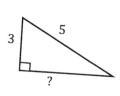

2)

3)
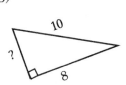

4)
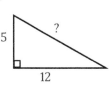

✎ Find the measure of the unknown angle in each triangle.

5)
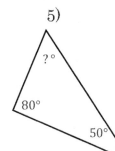

6)
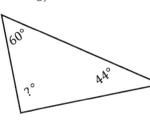

7)
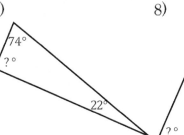

8)
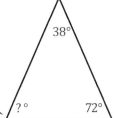

✎ Find the area of each triangle.

9)
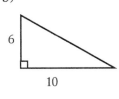

10)
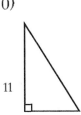

11)
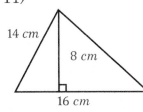

12)
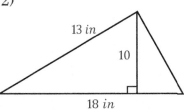

✎ Find the perimeter or circumference of each shape.

13)
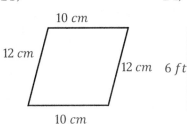

14)
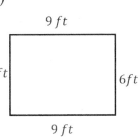

15)
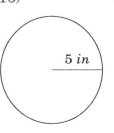

16) *regular hexagon*
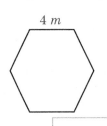

Effortless
Math
Education

✎ **Find the area of each trapezoid.**

17)   18)   19)   20)

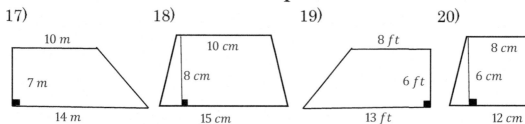

✎ **Find the volume of each cube.**

21)   22)   23)   24)

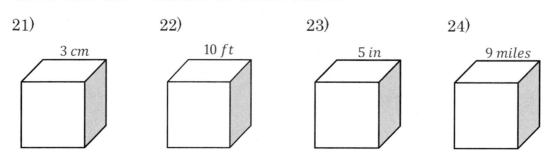

✎ **Find the volume of each Rectangular Prism.**

25)   26)   27)

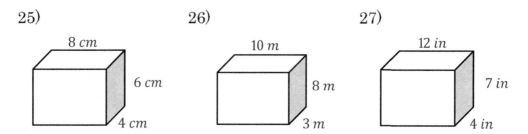

✎ **Find the volume of each Cylinder. Round your answer to the nearest tenth. ($\pi = 3.14$)**

28)   29)   30)

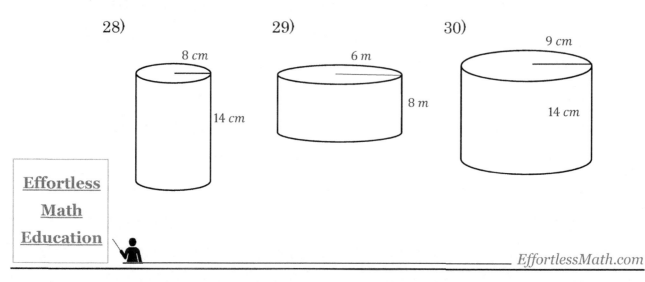

Effortless

Math

Education

Chapter 11: Answers

1) 4	11) $64\ cm^2$	21) $27\ cm^3$
2) 15	12) $90\ in^2$	22) $1{,}000\ ft^3$
3) 6	13) $44\ cm$	23) $125\ in^3$
4) 13	14) $30\ ft$	24) $729\ mi^3$
5) 50	15) $10\ \pi \approx 31.4\ in$	25) $192\ cm^3$
6) 76	16) $24\ m$	26) $240\ m^3$
7) 84	17) $84\ m^2$	27) $336\ in^3$
8) 70	18) $100\ cm^2$	28) $2{,}813.44\ cm^3$
9) 30	19) $63\ ft^2$	29) $904.32\ m^3$
10) 49.5	20) $60\ cm^2$	30) $3{,}560.76\ cm^3$

CHAPTER

12 Statistics

Math topics that you'll learn in this chapter:

- ☑ Mean, Median, Mode, and Range of the Given Data
- ☑ Pie Graph
- ☑ Probability Problems
- ☑ Permutations and Combinations

115

Mean, Median, Mode, and Range of the Given Data

- **Mean:** $\dfrac{sum\ of\ the\ data}{total\ number\ of\ data\ entires}$

- **Mode:** the value in the list that appears most often

- **Median:** is the middle number of a group of numbers arranged in order by size.

- **Range:** the difference of the largest value and smallest value in the list

Examples:

Example 1. What is the mode of these numbers? $5, 6, 8, 6, 8, 5, 3, 5$

Solution: Mode: the value in the list that appears most often.
Therefore, the mode is number 5. There are three number 5 in the data.

Example 2. What is the median of these numbers? $6, 11, 15, 10, 17, 20, 7$

Solution: Write the numbers in order: $6, 7, 10, 11, 15, 17, 20$
The median is the number in the middle. Therefore, the median is 11.

Example 3. What is the mean of these numbers? $7, 2, 3, 2, 4, 8, 7, 5$

Solution: Mean: $\dfrac{sum\ of\ the\ data}{total\ number\ of\ data\ entires} = \dfrac{7+2+3+2+4+8+7+5}{8} = \dfrac{38}{8} = 4.75$

Example 4. What is the range in this list? $3, 7, 12, 6, 15, 20, 8$

Solution: Range is the difference of the largest value and smallest value in the list. The largest value is 20 and the smallest value is 3.
Then: $20 - 3 = 17$

Pie Graph

- A Pie Graph (Pie Chart) is a circle chart divided into sectors, each sector represents the relative size of each value.

- Pie charts represent a snapshot of how a group is broken down into smaller pieces.

Examples:

A library has 750 books that include Mathematics, Physics, Chemistry, English and History. Use the following graph to answer the questions.

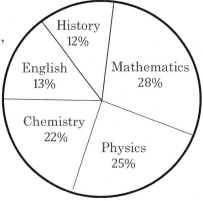

Example 1. What is the number of Mathematics books?

Solution: Number of total books = 750

Percent of Mathematics books = 28%

Then, the number of Mathematics books: 28% × 750 = 0.28 × 750 = 210

Example 2. What is the number of History books?

Solution: Number of total books = 750

Percent of History books = 12%

Then: 0.12 × 750 = 90

Example 3. What is the number of Chemistry books in the library?

Solution: Number of total books = 750

Percent of Chemistry books = 22%

Then: 0.22 × 750 = 165

Probability Problems

- Probability is the likelihood of something happening in the future. It is expressed as a number between zero (can never happen) to 1 (will always happen).

- Probability can be expressed as a fraction, a decimal, or a percent.

- Probability formula: $Probability = \frac{number\ of\ desired\ outcomes}{number\ of\ total\ outcomes}$

Examples:

Example 1. Anita's trick–or–treat bag contains 10 pieces of chocolate, 16 suckers, 16 pieces of gum, 22 pieces of licorice. If she randomly pulls a piece of candy from her bag, what is the probability of her pulling out a piece of sucker?

Solution: Probability $= \frac{number\ of\ desired\ outcomes}{number\ of\ total\ outcomes}$

Probability of pulling out a piece of sucker $= \frac{16}{10+16+16+22} = \frac{16}{64} = \frac{1}{4}$

Example 2. A bag contains 20 balls: four green, five black, eight blue, a brown, a red and one white. If 19 balls are removed from the bag at random, what is the probability that a brown ball has been removed?

Solution: If 19 balls are removed from the bag at random, there will be one ball in the bag. The probability of choosing a brown ball is 1 out of 20. Therefore, the probability of not choosing a brown ball is 19 out of 20 and the probability of having not a brown ball after removing 19 balls is the same. The answer is: $\frac{19}{20}$

Permutations and Combinations

Factorials are products, indicated by an exclamation mark. For example, $4! = 4 \times 3 \times 2 \times 1$ (Remember that 0! is defined to be equal to 1)

- **Permutations:** The number of ways to choose a sample of k elements from a set of n distinct objects where order does matter, and replacements are not allowed. For a permutation problem, use this formula:

$$_nP_k = \frac{n!}{(n-k)!}$$

- **Combination:** The number of ways to choose a sample of r elements from a set of n distinct objects where order does not matter, and replacements are not allowed. For a combination problem, use this formula:

$$_nC_r = \frac{n!}{r!\,(n-r)!}$$

Examples:

Example 1. How many ways can the first and second place be awarded to 7 people?

Solution: Since the order matters, (the first and second place are different!) we need to use permutation formula where n is 7 and k is 2. Then: $\frac{n!}{(n-k)!} = \frac{7!}{(7-2)!} = \frac{7!}{5!} = \frac{7 \times 6 \times 5!}{5!}$, remove 5! from both sides of the fraction. Then: $\frac{7 \times 6 \times 5!}{5!} = 7 \times 6 = 42$

Example 2. How many ways can we pick a team of 3 people from a group of 8?

Solution: Since the order doesn't matter, we need to use a combination formula where n is 8 and r is 3.

Then: $\frac{n!}{r!\,(n-r)!} = \frac{8!}{3!\,(8-3)!} = \frac{8!}{3!\,(5)!} = \frac{8 \times 7 \times 6 \times 5!}{3!\,(5)!} = \frac{8 \times 7 \times 6}{3 \times 2 \times 1} = \frac{336}{6} = 56$

Chapter 12: Practices

✎ Find the values of the Given Data.

1) $6, 11, 5, 3, 6$

Mode: _____   Range: _____

Mean: _____   Median: _____

2) $4, 9, 1, 9, 6, 7$

Mode: _____   Range: _____

Mean: _____   Median: _____

3) $10, 3, 6, 10, 4, 15$

Mode: _____   Range: _____

Mean: _____   Median: _____

4) $12, 4, 8, 9, 3, 12, 15$

Mode: _____   Range: _____

Mean: _____   Median: _____

✎ The circle graph below shows all Bob's expenses for last month. Bob spent $790 on his Rent last month.

5) How much did Bob's total expenses last month? _____

6) How much did Bob spend for foods last month? _____

7) How much did Bob spend for his bills last month? _____

8) How much did Bob spend on his car last month? _____

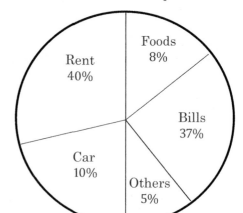

Bob's last month expenses

Effortless Math Education

🖎 Solve.

9) Bag A contains 8 red marbles and 6 green marbles. Bag B contains 5 black marbles and 7 orange marbles. What is the probability of selecting a green marble at random from bag A? What is the probability of selecting a black marble at random from Bag B?

_____   _____

🖎 Solve.

10) Susan is baking cookies. She uses sugar, flour, butter, and eggs. How many different orders of ingredients can she try? _____

11) Jason is planning for his vacation. He wants to go to museum, go to the beach, and play volleyball. How many different ways of ordering are there for him? _____

12) In how many ways can a team of 6 basketball players choose a captain and co-captain? _____

13) How many ways can you give 5 balls to your 8 friends? _____

14) A professor is going to arrange her 5 students in a straight line. In how many ways can she do this? _____

15) In how many ways can a teacher chooses 12 out of 15 students?

_____

Effortless Math Education

Chapter 12: Answers

1) Mode: 6, Range: 8, Mean: 6.2, Median: 6

2) Mode: 9, Range:8, Mean: 6, Median: 6.5

3) Mode: 10, Range: 12, Mean: 8, Median: 8

4) Mode: 12, Range: 12, Mean: 9, Median: 9

5) $1,975

6) $158

7) $730.75

8) $197.50

9) $\frac{3}{7}, \frac{5}{12}$

10) 24

11) 6

12) 30 (it's a permutation problem)

13) 56 (it's a combination problem)

14) 120

15) 455 (it's a combination problem)

13 Functions Operations

Math topics that you'll learn in this chapter:

- ☑ Function Notation and Evaluation
- ☑ Adding and Subtracting Functions
- ☑ Multiplying and Dividing Functions
- ☑ Composition of Functions

123

Function Notation and Evaluation

- Functions are mathematical operations that assign unique outputs to given inputs.

- Function notation is the way a function is written. It is meant to be a precise way of giving information about the function without a rather lengthy written explanation.

- The most popular function notation is $f(x)$ which is read "f of x". Any letter can name a function. for example: $g(x)$, $h(x)$, etc.

- To evaluate a function, plug in the input (the given value or expression) for the function's variable (place holder, x).

Examples:

Example 1. Evaluate: $f(x) = x + 6$, find $f(2)$

Solution: Substitute x with 2:
Then: $f(x) = x + 6 \rightarrow f(2) = 2 + 6 \rightarrow f(2) = 8$

Example 2. Evaluate: $w(x) = 3x - 1$, find $w(4)$.

Solution: Substitute x with 4:
Then: $w(x) = 3x - 1 \rightarrow w(4) = 3(4) - 1 = 12 - 1 = 11$

Example 3. Evaluate: $f(x) = 2x^2 + 4$, find $f(-1)$.

Solution: Substitute x with -1:
Then: $f(x) = 2x^2 + 4 \rightarrow f(-1) = 2(-1)^2 + 4 \rightarrow f(-1) = 2 + 4 = 6$

Example 4. Evaluate: $h(x) = 4x^2 - 9$, find $h(2a)$.

Solution: Substitute x with $2a$:
Then: $h(x) = 4x^2 - 9 \rightarrow h(2a) = 4(2a)^2 - 9 \rightarrow h(2a) = 4(4a^2) - 9 = 16a^2 - 9$

Adding and Subtracting Functions

- Just like we can add and subtract numbers and expressions, we can add or subtract functions and simplify or evaluate them. The result is a new function.

- For two functions $f(x)$ and $g(x)$, we can create two new functions:

$$(f + g)(x) = f(x) + g(x) \text{ and } (f - g)(x) = f(x) - g(x)$$

Examples:

Example 1. $g(x) = 2x - 2$, $f(x) = x + 1$, Find: $(g + f)(x)$

Solution: $(g + f)(x) = g(x) + f(x)$
Then: $(g + f)(x) = (2x - 2) + (x + 1) = 2x - 2 + x + 1 = 3x - 1$

Example 2. $f(x) = 4x - 3$, $g(x) = 2x - 4$, Find: $(f - g)(x)$

Solution: $(f - g)(x) = f(x) - g(x)$
Then: $(f - g)(x) = (4x - 3) - (2x - 4) = 4x - 3 - 2x + 4 = 2x + 1$

Example 3. $g(x) = x^2 + 2$, $f(x) = x + 5$, Find: $(g + f)(x)$

Solution: $(g + f)(x) = g(x) + f(x)$
Then: $(g + f)(x) = (x^2 + 2) + (x + 5) = x^2 + x + 7$

Example 4. $f(x) = 5x^2 - 3$, $g(x) = 3x + 6$, Find: $(f - g)(3)$

Solution: $(f - g)(x) = f(x) - g(x)$
Then: $(f - g)(x) = (5x^2 - 3) - (3x + 6) = 5x^2 - 3 - 3x - 6 = 5x^2 - 3x - 9$
Substitute x with 3: $(f - g)(3) = 5(3)^2 - 3(3) - 9 = 45 - 9 - 9 = 27$

Multiplying and Dividing Functions

- Just like we can multiply and divide numbers and expressions, we can multiply and divide two functions and simplify or evaluate them.

- For two functions $f(x)$ and $g(x)$, we can create two new functions:

$$(f.g)(x) = f(x).g(x) \text{ and } \left(\frac{f}{g}\right)(x) = \frac{f(x)}{g(x)}$$

Examples:

Example 1. $g(x) = x + 3$, $f(x) = x + 4$, Find: $(g.f)(x)$

Solution:

$$(g.f)(x) = g(x).f(x) = (x+3)(x+4) = x^2 + 4x + 3x + 12 = x^2 + 7x + 12$$

Example 2. $f(x) = x + 6$, $h(x) = x - 9$, Find: $\left(\frac{f}{h}\right)(x)$

Solution: $\left(\frac{f}{h}\right)(x) = \frac{f(x)}{h(x)} = \frac{x+6}{x-9}$

Example 3. $g(x) = x + 7$, $f(x) = x - 3$, Find: $(g.f)(2)$

Solution: $(g.f)(x) = g(x).f(x) = (x+7)(x-3) = x^2 - 3x + 7x - 21$

$$g(x).f(x) = x^2 + 4x - 21$$

Substitute x with 2: $(g.f)(x) = (2)^2 + 4(2) - 21 = 4 + 8 - 21 = -9$

Example 4. $f(x) = x + 3$, $h(x) = 2x - 4$, Find: $\left(\frac{f}{h}\right)(3)$

Solution: $\left(\frac{f}{h}\right)(x) = \frac{f(x)}{h(x)} = \frac{x+3}{2x-4}$

Substitute x with 3: $\left(\frac{f}{h}\right)(x) = \frac{x+3}{2x-4} = \frac{3+3}{2(3)-4} = \frac{6}{2} = 3$

Composition of Functions

- "Composition of functions" simply means combining two or more functions in a way where the output from one function becomes the input for the next function.

- The notation used for composition is: $(fog)(x) = f(g(x))$ and is read "f composed with g of x" or "f of g of x".

Examples:

Example 1. Using $f(x) = 2x + 3$ and $g(x) = 5x$, find: $(fog)(x)$

Solution: $(fog)(x) = f(g(x))$. Then: $(fog)(x) = f(g(x)) = f(5x)$

Now find $f(5x)$ by substituting x with $5x$ in $f(x)$ function.

Then: $f(x) = 2x + 3$; $(x \to 5x) \to f(5x) = 2(5x) + 3 = 10x + 3$

Example 2. Using $f(x) = 3x - 1$ and $g(x) = 2x - 2$, find: $(gof)(5)$

Solution: $(fog)(x) = f(g(x))$. Then: $(gof)(x) = g(f(x)) = g(3x - 1)$,

Now substitute x in $g(x)$ by $(3x - 1)$.

Then: $g(3x - 1) = 2(3x - 1) - 2 = 6x - 2 - 2 = 6x - 4$

Substitute x with 5: $(gof)(5) = g(f(x)) = 6x - 4 = 6(5) - 4 = 26$

Example 3. Using $f(x) = 2x^2 - 5$ and $g(x) = x + 3$, find: $f(g(3))$

Solution: First, find $g(3)$: $g(x) = x + 3 \to g(3) = 3 + 3 = 6$

Then: $f(g(3)) = f(6)$. Now, find $f(6)$ by substituting x with 6 in $f(x)$ function.

$f(g(3)) = f(6) = 2(6)^2 - 5 = 2(36) - 5 = 67$

Chapter 13: Practices

✍ Evaluate each function.

1) $g(n) = 2n + 5$, find $g(2)$

____

2) $h(x) = 5x - 9$, find $h(4)$

____

3) $k(n) = 10 - 6n$, find $k(2)$

____

4) $g(x) = -5x + 6$, find $g(-2)$

____

5) $k(n) = -8n + 3$, find $k(-6)$

____

6) $w(n) = -2n - 9$, find $w(-5)$

____

✍ Perform the indicated operation.

7) $f(x) = x + 6$

$g(x) = 3x + 2$

Find $(f - g)(x)$

____

8) $g(x) = x - 9$

$f(x) = 2x - 1$

Find $(g - f)(x)$

____

9) $h(t) = 5t + 6$

$g(t) = 2t + 4$

Find $(h + g)(x)$

____

10) $g(a) = -6a + 1$

$f(a) = 3a^2 - 3$

Find $(g + f)(5)$

____

11) $g(x) = 7x - 1$

$h(x) = -4x^2 + 2$

Find $(g - h)(-3)$

____

12) $h(x) = -x^2 - 1$

$g(x) = -7x - 1$

Find $(h - g)(-5)$

____

✍ Perform the indicated operation.

13) $g(x) = x + 3$

$f(x) = x + 1$

Find $(g.f)(x)$

_____

14) $f(x) = 4x$

$h(x) = x - 6$

Find $(f.h)(x)$

_____

15) $g(a) = a - 8$

$h(a) = 4a - 2$

Find $(g.h)(3)$

_____

16) $f(x) = 6x + 2$

$h(x) = 5x - 1$

Find $\left(\frac{f}{h}\right)(-2)$

_____

17) $f(x) = 7a - 1$

$g(x) = -5 - 2a$

Find $\left(\frac{f}{g}\right)(-4)$

_____

18) $g(a) = a^2 - 4$

$f(a) = a + 6$

Find $\left(\frac{g}{f}\right)(-3)$

_____

✍ Using $f(x) = 4x + 3$ and $g(x) = x - 7$, find:

19) $g\big(f(2)\big) =$ _____

20) $g\big(f(-2)\big) =$ _____

21) $f\big(g(4)\big) =$ _____

22) $f\big(f(7)\big) =$ _____

23) $g\big(f(5)\big) =$ _____

24) $g\big(f(-5)\big) =$ _____

25) $g\big(f(7)\big) =$ _____

26) $g\big(f(-3)\big) =$ _____

27) $f\big(g(-6)\big) =$ _____

Effortless
Math
Education

Chapter 13: Answers

1)   9

2)   11

3) -2

4)   16

5)   51

6)   1

7) $-2x + 4$

8) $-x - 8$

9) $7t + 10$

10) 43

11) 12

12) -60

13) $x^2 + 4x + 3$

14) $4x^2 - 24x$

15) -50

16) $\frac{10}{11}$

17) $-\frac{29}{3}$

18) $\frac{5}{3}$

19) 4

20) -12

21) -9

22) 127

23) 16

24) -24

25) 24

26) -16

27) -49

Effortless Math Education

Math Practice Tests

Time to refine your skill with a practice examination

In this section, there are 2 complete Math Practice Tests. Take these tests to simulate the test day experience. After you've finished, score your tests using the answer keys.

Before You Start

- You'll need a pencil, a calculator and scratch papers to take the test.
- For each question, there are four possible answers. Choose which one is best.
- It's okay to guess. There is no penalty for wrong answers.
- Use the answer sheet provided to record your answers.
- After you've finished the test, review the answer key to see where you went wrong.

Good Luck!

The hardest arithmetic to master is that which enables us to count our blessings. ~Eric Hoffer

Math Practice
Test 1

2024

Total number of questions: 50

Total time: No time limit

Basic Calculator is permitted for Math Practice Test.

Math Practice Test Answer Sheet

Remove (or photocopy) this answer sheet and use it to complete the practice test.

	Math Practice Test 1		
1 Ⓐ Ⓑ Ⓒ Ⓓ	16 Ⓐ Ⓑ Ⓒ Ⓓ	31 Ⓐ Ⓑ Ⓒ Ⓓ	46 Ⓐ Ⓑ Ⓒ Ⓓ
2 Ⓐ Ⓑ Ⓒ Ⓓ	17 Ⓐ Ⓑ Ⓒ Ⓓ	32 Ⓐ Ⓑ Ⓒ Ⓓ	47 Ⓐ Ⓑ Ⓒ Ⓓ
3 Ⓐ Ⓑ Ⓒ Ⓓ	18 Ⓐ Ⓑ Ⓒ Ⓓ	33 Ⓐ Ⓑ Ⓒ Ⓓ	48 Ⓐ Ⓑ Ⓒ Ⓓ
4 Ⓐ Ⓑ Ⓒ Ⓓ	19 Ⓐ Ⓑ Ⓒ Ⓓ	34 Ⓐ Ⓑ Ⓒ Ⓓ	39 Ⓐ Ⓑ Ⓒ Ⓓ
5 Ⓐ Ⓑ Ⓒ Ⓓ	20 Ⓐ Ⓑ Ⓒ Ⓓ	35 Ⓐ Ⓑ Ⓒ Ⓓ	50 Ⓐ Ⓑ Ⓒ Ⓓ
6 Ⓐ Ⓑ Ⓒ Ⓓ	21 Ⓐ Ⓑ Ⓒ Ⓓ	36 Ⓐ Ⓑ Ⓒ Ⓓ	
7 Ⓐ Ⓑ Ⓒ Ⓓ	22 Ⓐ Ⓑ Ⓒ Ⓓ	37 Ⓐ Ⓑ Ⓒ Ⓓ	
8 Ⓐ Ⓑ Ⓒ Ⓓ	23 Ⓐ Ⓑ Ⓒ Ⓓ	38 Ⓐ Ⓑ Ⓒ Ⓓ	
9 Ⓐ Ⓑ Ⓒ Ⓓ	24 Ⓐ Ⓑ Ⓒ Ⓓ	39 Ⓐ Ⓑ Ⓒ Ⓓ	
10 Ⓐ Ⓑ Ⓒ Ⓓ	25 Ⓐ Ⓑ Ⓒ Ⓓ	40 Ⓐ Ⓑ Ⓒ Ⓓ	
11 Ⓐ Ⓑ Ⓒ Ⓓ	26 Ⓐ Ⓑ Ⓒ Ⓓ	41 Ⓐ Ⓑ Ⓒ Ⓓ	
12 Ⓐ Ⓑ Ⓒ Ⓓ	27 Ⓐ Ⓑ Ⓒ Ⓓ	42 Ⓐ Ⓑ Ⓒ Ⓓ	
13 Ⓐ Ⓑ Ⓒ Ⓓ	28 Ⓐ Ⓑ Ⓒ Ⓓ	43 Ⓐ Ⓑ Ⓒ Ⓓ	
14 Ⓐ Ⓑ Ⓒ Ⓓ	29 Ⓐ Ⓑ Ⓒ Ⓓ	44 Ⓐ Ⓑ Ⓒ Ⓓ	
15 Ⓐ Ⓑ Ⓒ Ⓓ	30 Ⓐ Ⓑ Ⓒ Ⓓ	45 Ⓐ Ⓑ Ⓒ Ⓓ	

1) The mean of 50 test scores was calculated as 90. But, it turned out that one of the scores was misread as 94 but it was 69. What is the mean?

A. 85

B. 87

C. 89.5

D. 90.5

2) Two dice are thrown simultaneously, what is the probability of getting a sum of 5 or 8?

A. $\frac{1}{3}$

B. $\frac{11}{36}$

C. $\frac{1}{16}$

D. $\frac{1}{4}$

3) Which of the following is equal to the expression below?

$$(5x + 2y)(2x - y)$$

A. $4x^2 - 2y^2$

B. $2x^2 + 6xy - 2y^2$

C. $24x^2 + 2xy - 2y^2$

D. $10x^2 - xy - 2y^2$

4) What is the product of all possible values of x in the following equation?

$$|x - 10| = 4$$

A. 3

B. 7

C. 13

D. 84

5) What is the slope of a line that is perpendicular to the line $4x - 2y = 6$?

A. -2

B. $-\frac{1}{2}$

C. 4

D. 12

6) What is the value of the expression $6(x - 2y) + (2 - x)^2$ when $x = 3$ and $y = -2$?

A. -4

B. 20

C. 43

D. 50

7) A swimming pool holds 2,500 cubic feet of water. The swimming pool is 25 feet long and 10 feet wide. How deep is the swimming pool?

A. $2\ feet$

B. $4\ feet$

C. $6\ feet$

D. $10\ feet$

8) Four one – foot rulers can be split among how many users to leave each with $\frac{1}{3}$ of a ruler?

A. 4

B. 6

C. 12

D. 24

9) What is the area of a square whose diagonal is 4?

A. 4

B. 8

C. 16

D. 64

10) The average of five numbers is 26. If a sixth number 42 is added, then, what is the new average? (round your answer to the nearest hundredth)

A. 25

B. 26.5

C. 27

D. 28.66

Questions 11 to 13 are based on the following data

The result of a research shows the number of men and women in four cities of a country.

Number of men and women in four cities

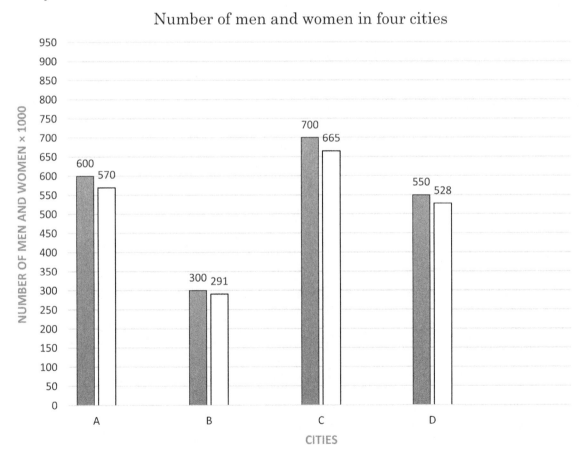

11) What's the maximum ratio of the number of women to number of men in each city?

A. 0.98

B. 0.97

C. 0.96

D. 0.95

12) What's the ratio of the percentage of men in city A to percentage of women in city C?

A. $\frac{10}{9}$

B. $\frac{9}{10}$

C. 1

D. $\frac{20}{19}$

13) How many women should be added to city D to change the ratio of women to men to 1.2?

A. 130

B. 129

C. 132

D. 131

14) Jason needs an 70% average in his writing class to pass. On his first 4 exams, he earned scores of 68%, 72%, 85%, and 90%. What is the minimum score Jason can earn on his fifth and final test to pass?

A. 80%,

B. 70%

C. 68%

D. 35%

15) What is the value of x in the following equation? $\frac{2}{3}x + \frac{1}{6} = \frac{1}{2}$

A. 6

B. $\frac{1}{2}$

C. $\frac{1}{3}$

D. $\frac{1}{4}$

16) A bank is offering 4.5% simple interest on a savings account. If you deposit $12,000, how much interest will you earn in two years?

A. $420

B. $1,080

C. $4,200

D. $8,400

17) Simplify $7x^2y^3(2x^2y)^3 =$

A. $12x^4y^6$

B. $12x^8y^6$

C. $56x^4y^6$

D. $56x^8y^6$

18) What is the surface area of the cylinder below?

A. $40\,\pi\ in^2$

B. $57\,\pi\ in^2$

C. $66\,\pi\ in^2$

D. $288\,\pi\ in^2$

E. $400\,\pi\ in^2$

19) Last week 25,000 fans attended a football match. This week three times as many bought tickets, but one sixth of them cancelled their tickets. How many are attending this week?

A. 48,000

B. 54,000

C. 62,500

D. 75,000

20) What is the perimeter of a square that has an area of 49 square inches?

A. 144 *inches*

B. 64 *inches*

C. 56 *inches*

D. 28 *inches*

21) If $f(x) = 2x^3 + 5x^2 + 2x$ and $g(x) = -4$, what is the value of $f(g(x))$?

A. 56

B. 32

C. 24

D. -56

22) A cruise line ship left Port A and traveled 50 miles due west and then 120 miles due north. At this point, what is the shortest distance from the cruise to port A?

A. 70 *miles*

B. 80 *miles*

C. 150 *miles*

D. 130 *miles*

23) What is the equivalent temperature of 104°F in Celsius?

$$C = \frac{5}{9}(F - 32)$$

A. 32

B. 40

C. 48

D. 52

24) The perimeter of a rectangular yard is 72 meters. What is its length if its width is twice its length?

A. 12 *meters*

B. 18 *meters*

C. 20 *meters*

D. 24 *meters*

25) The average of 6 numbers is 14. The average of 4 of those numbers is 10. What is the average of the other two numbers?

A. 10

B. 12

C. 14

D. 22

26) If 150% of a number is 75, then what is the 80% of that number?

A. 40

B. 50

C. 70

D. 85

27) What is the slope of the line: $4x - 2y = 12$

A. -1

B. -2

C. 1

D. 2

28) In two successive years, the population of a town is increased by 10% and 20%. What percent of the population is increased after two years?

A. 30%

B. 32%

C. 35%

D. 68%

29) The area of a circle is 36π. What is the diameter of the circle?

A. 4

B. 8

C. 12

D. 14

30) If 20% of a number is 4, what is the number?

A. 4

B. 8

C. 10

D. 20

31) If a tree casts a 26–foot shadow at the same time that a 3 feet yardstick casts a 2–foot shadow, what is the height of the tree?

A. 24 ft

B. 28 ft

C. 39 ft

D. 48 ft

32) Jason is 9 miles ahead of Joe running at 6.5 miles per hour and Joe is running at the speed of 8 miles per hour. How long does it take Joe to catch Jason?

A. 3 $hours$

B. 4 $hours$

C. 6 $hours$

D. 8 $hours$

33) 44 students took an exam and 11 of them failed. What percent of the students passed the exam?

A. 20%

B. 40%

C. 60%

D. 75%

34) If $f(x) = 2x^3 + 5x^2 + 2x$ and $g(x) = -3$, what is the value of $f(g(x))$?

A. 36

B. 32

C. 24

D. −15

35) The diagonal of a rectangle is 10 inches long and the height of the rectangle is 6 inches. What is the perimeter of the rectangle?

A. 10 *inches*

B. 12 *inches*

C. 16 *inches*

D. 28 *inches*

36) The perimeter of the trapezoid below (not drawn to scale) is 38 *cm*. What is its area?

A. 48 cm^2

B. 78 cm^2

C. 140 cm^2

D. 576 cm^2

13 cm

4 cm

9 cm

37) If $f(x) = 2x^3 + 2$ and $(x) = \frac{1}{x}$, what is the value of $f(g(x))$?

A. $\frac{1}{2x^3 + 2}$

B. $\frac{2}{x^3}$

C. $\frac{1}{2x}$

D. $\frac{2}{x^3} + 2$

38) A cruise line ship left Port *A* and traveled 80 miles due west and then 150 miles due north. At this point, what is the shortest distance from the cruise to port *A*?

A. 70 miles

B. 80 miles

C. 150 miles

D. 170 miles

39) If the ratio of $5a$ to $2b$ is $\frac{1}{10}$, what is the ratio of a to b?

A. 10

B. 25

C. $\frac{1}{25}$

D. $\frac{1}{20}$

40) If $x = 9$, what is the value of y in the following equation? $2y = \frac{2x^2}{3} + 6$

A. 30

B. 45

C. 60

D. 120

41) If $\frac{x-3}{5} = N$ and $N = 6$, what is the value of x?

A. 25

B. 28

C. 30

D. 33

42) Which of the following is equal to $b^{\frac{3}{5}}$?

A. $\sqrt{b^{\frac{5}{3}}}$

B. $b^{\frac{5}{3}}$

C. $\sqrt[5]{b^3}$

D. $\sqrt[3]{b^5}$

43) On Saturday, Sara read N pages of a book each hour for 3 hours, and Mary read M pages of a book each hour for 4 hours. Which of the following represents the total number of pages of book read by Sara and Mary on Saturday?

A. $12MN$

B. $3N + 4M$

C. $7MN$

D. $4N + 3M$

44) Sara opened a bank account that earns 2 percent compounded annually. Her initial deposit was \$150, and she uses the expression $\$150(x)^n$ to find the value of the account after n years. What is the value of x in the expression?

A. 0.02

B. 0.20

C. 20%

D. 1.02

45) If function is defined as $f(x) = bx^2 + 15$, and b is a constant and $f(2) = 35$. What is the value of $f(5)$?

A. 25

B. 35

C. 140

D. 165

46) Find the solution (x, y) to the following system of equations?
$$2x + 5y = 11$$
$$4x - 2y = -14$$

A. $(14, 5)$

B. $(6, 8)$

C. $(11, 17)$

D. $(-2, 3)$

47) Calculate $f(4)$ for the function $f(x) = 3x^2 - 4$.

A. 44

B. 40

C. 38

D. 30

48) What are the zeroes of the function $f(x) = x^3 + 5x^2 + 6x$?

A. 0

B. 2

C. $0, 2, 3$

D. $0, -2, -3$

49) Which of the following lines is parallel to: $6y - 2x = 24$?

A. $y = \frac{1}{3}x + 2$

B. $y = 3x + 5$

C. $y = x - 2$

D. $y = 2x - 1$

50) The average of $13, 15, 20$ and x is 20. What is the value of x?

A. 9

B. 15

C. 18

D. 32

End of Math Practice Test 1.

Math Practice
Test 2

2024

Total number of questions: 50

Total time: No time limit

Basic Calculator is permitted for Math Practice Test.

Math Practice Test Answer Sheet

Remove (or photocopy) this answer sheet and use it to complete the practice test.

Math Practice Test 2			
1 Ⓐ Ⓑ Ⓒ Ⓓ	16 Ⓐ Ⓑ Ⓒ Ⓓ	31 Ⓐ Ⓑ Ⓒ Ⓓ	46 Ⓐ Ⓑ Ⓒ Ⓓ
2 Ⓐ Ⓑ Ⓒ Ⓓ	17 Ⓐ Ⓑ Ⓒ Ⓓ	32 Ⓐ Ⓑ Ⓒ Ⓓ	47 Ⓐ Ⓑ Ⓒ Ⓓ
3 Ⓐ Ⓑ Ⓒ Ⓓ	18 Ⓐ Ⓑ Ⓒ Ⓓ	33 Ⓐ Ⓑ Ⓒ Ⓓ	48 Ⓐ Ⓑ Ⓒ Ⓓ
4 Ⓐ Ⓑ Ⓒ Ⓓ	19 Ⓐ Ⓑ Ⓒ Ⓓ	34 Ⓐ Ⓑ Ⓒ Ⓓ	39 Ⓐ Ⓑ Ⓒ Ⓓ
5 Ⓐ Ⓑ Ⓒ Ⓓ	20 Ⓐ Ⓑ Ⓒ Ⓓ	35 Ⓐ Ⓑ Ⓒ Ⓓ	50 Ⓐ Ⓑ Ⓒ Ⓓ
6 Ⓐ Ⓑ Ⓒ Ⓓ	21 Ⓐ Ⓑ Ⓒ Ⓓ	36 Ⓐ Ⓑ Ⓒ Ⓓ	
7 Ⓐ Ⓑ Ⓒ Ⓓ	22 Ⓐ Ⓑ Ⓒ Ⓓ	37 Ⓐ Ⓑ Ⓒ Ⓓ	
8 Ⓐ Ⓑ Ⓒ Ⓓ	23 Ⓐ Ⓑ Ⓒ Ⓓ	38 Ⓐ Ⓑ Ⓒ Ⓓ	
9 Ⓐ Ⓑ Ⓒ Ⓓ	24 Ⓐ Ⓑ Ⓒ Ⓓ	39 Ⓐ Ⓑ Ⓒ Ⓓ	
10 Ⓐ Ⓑ Ⓒ Ⓓ	25 Ⓐ Ⓑ Ⓒ Ⓓ	40 Ⓐ Ⓑ Ⓒ Ⓓ	
11 Ⓐ Ⓑ Ⓒ Ⓓ	26 Ⓐ Ⓑ Ⓒ Ⓓ	41 Ⓐ Ⓑ Ⓒ Ⓓ	
12 Ⓐ Ⓑ Ⓒ Ⓓ	27 Ⓐ Ⓑ Ⓒ Ⓓ	42 Ⓐ Ⓑ Ⓒ Ⓓ	
13 Ⓐ Ⓑ Ⓒ Ⓓ	28 Ⓐ Ⓑ Ⓒ Ⓓ	43 Ⓐ Ⓑ Ⓒ Ⓓ	
14 Ⓐ Ⓑ Ⓒ Ⓓ	29 Ⓐ Ⓑ Ⓒ Ⓓ	44 Ⓐ Ⓑ Ⓒ Ⓓ	
15 Ⓐ Ⓑ Ⓒ Ⓓ	30 Ⓐ Ⓑ Ⓒ Ⓓ	45 Ⓐ Ⓑ Ⓒ Ⓓ	

1) When a number is subtracted from 24 and the difference is divided by that number, the result is 3. What is the value of the number?

A. 2

B. 4

C. 6

D. 12

2) An angle is equal to one fifth of its supplement. What is the measure of that angle?

A. 20

B. 30

C. 45

D. 60

3) John traveled 150 km in 6 hours and Alice traveled 180 km in 4 hours. What is the ratio of the average speed of John to average speed of Alice?

A. 3 : 2

B. 2 : 3

C. 5 : 9

D. 5 : 6

4) If 40% of a class are girls, and 35% of girls play tennis, what percent of the class play tennis?

A. 10%

B. 14%

C. 20%

D. 40%

5) If the interior angles of a quadrilateral are in the ratio 1: 2: 3: 4, what is the measure of the smallest angle?

A. 36°

B. 72°

C. 108°

D. 144°

6) How long does a 420–miles trip take moving at 50 miles per hour (*mph*)?

A. 4 *hours*

B. 6 *hours and* 24 *minutes*

C. 8 *hours and* 24 *minutes*

D. 8 *hours and* 30 *minutes*

7) Right triangle *ABC* has two legs of lengths 6 *cm* (*AB*) and 8 *cm* (*AC*). What is the length of the third side (*BC*)?

A. 4 *cm*

B. 6 *cm*

C. 8 *cm*

D. 10 *cm*

8) The ratio of boys to girls in a school is 2: 3. If there are 600 students in a school, how many boys are in the school.

A. 540

B. 360

C. 300

D. 240

9) 25 is what percent of 20?

A. 20%

B. 25%

C. 125%

D. 150%

10) The perimeter of the trapezoid below (not drawn to scale) is 56. What is its area?

A. 252 cm^2

B. 234 cm^2

C. 216 cm^2

D. 180 cm^2

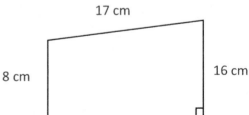

11) Two third of 18 is equal to $\frac{2}{5}$ of what number?

A. 12

B. 20

C. 30

D. 60

12) The marked price of a computer is D dollar. Its price decreased by 20% in January and later increased by 10% in February. What is the final price of the computer in D dollar?

A. 0.80 D

B. 0.88 D

C. 0.90 D

D. 1.20 D

13) The area of a circle is 25 π. What is the circumference of the circle?

A. 5 π

B. 10 π

C. 32 π

D. 64 π

14) In 1999, the average worker's income increased $3,000 per year starting from $24,000 annual salary. Which equation represents income greater than average? (I = income, x = number of years after 1999)

A. $I > 3,000\,x + 24,000$

B. $I > -3,000\,x + 24,000$

C. $I < -3,000\,x + 24,000$

D. $I < 3,000\,x - 24,000$

15) From last year, the price of gasoline has increased from $1.25 per gallon to $1.75 per gallon. The new price is what percent of the original price?

A. 72%

B. 120%

C. 140%

D. 160%

16) A boat sails 40 miles south and then 30 miles east. How far is the boat from its start point?

A. 45 *miles*

B. 50 *miles*

C. 60 *miles*

D. 70 *miles*

17) Sophia purchased a sofa for $530.40. The sofa is regularly priced at $624. What was the percent discount Sophia received on the sofa?

A. 12%

B. 15%

C. 20%

D. 25%

18) The score of Emma was half as that of Ava and the score of Mia was twice that of Ava. If the score of Mia was 60, what is the score of Emma?

A. 12

B. 15

C. 20

D. 30

19) The average of five consecutive numbers is 38. What is the smallest number?

A. 38

B. 36

C. 34

D. 12

20) How many tiles of 8 cm^2 is needed to cover a floor of dimension 6 cm by 24 cm?

A. 6

B. 12

C. 18

D. 24

21) A rope weighs 600 grams per meter of length. What is the weight in kilograms of 12.2 meters of this rope? (1 $kilograms = 1000 \ grams$)

A. 0.0732

B. 0.732

C. 7.32

D. 7,320

22) A chemical solution contains 4% alcohol. If there is 24 ml of alcohol, what is the volume of the solution?

A. 240 ml

B. 480 ml

C. 600 ml

D. 1,200 ml

23) The average weight of 18 girls in a class is 60 kg and the average weight of 32 boys in the same class is 62 kg. What is the average weight of all the 50 students in that class?

A. 60

B. 61.28

C. 61.68

D. 61.90

24) The price of a laptop is decreased by 10% to $360. What is its original price?

A. $320

B. $380

C. $400

D. $450

25) The radius of a cylinder is 8 inches and its height is 12 inches. What is the surface area of the cylinder?

A. 64 $\pi \ in^2$

B. 128 $\pi \ in^2$

C. 192 $\pi \ in^2$

D. 320 $\pi \ in^2$

26) The average of $13, 15, 20$ and x is 18. What is the value of x?

A. 9

B. 15

C. 18

D. 24

27) The price of a sofa is decreased by 25% to $420. What was its original price?

A. $480

B. $520

C. $560

D. $600

28) A bank is offering 4.5% simple interest on a savings account. If you deposit $8,000, how much interest will you earn in five years?

A. $360

B. $720

C. $1,800

D. $3,600

29) Multiply and write the product in scientific notation:

$$(4.2 \times 10^6) \times (2.6 \times 10^{-5})$$

A. 1092×10

B. 10.92×10^6

C. 109.2×10^{-5}

D. 1.092×10^2

30) If the height of a right pyramid is $12 \, cm$ and its base is a square with side $6 \, cm$. What is its volume?

A. $32 \, cm^3$

B. $36 \, cm^3$

C. $48 \, cm^3$

D. $144 \, cm^3$

31) Solve for x: $4(x + 1) = 6(x - 4) + 20$

A. 12

B. 8

C. 6.2

D. 4

32) Which of the following expressions is equivalent to $2x(4 + 2y)$?

A. 2xy + 8x

B. 8xy + 8x

C. xy + 8

D. 4xy + 8x

33) If $y = 4ab + 3b^3$, what is y when $a = 2$ and $b = 3$?

A. 24

B. 31

C. 36

D. 105

34) Which of the following graphs represents the compound inequality $-2 \leq 2x - 4 < 8$?

A.

B.

C.

D.

35) A number is chosen at random from 1 to 25. Find the probability of not selecting a composite number.

A. $\frac{9}{25}$

B. 25

C. $\frac{2}{5}$

D. 1

36) Which of the following points lies on the line $2x + 4y = 10$

A. $(2, 1)$

B. $(-1, 3)$

C. $(-2, 2)$

D. $(2, 2)$

37) The price of a car was $20,000 in 2014, $16,000 in 2015 and $12,800 in 2016. What is the rate of depreciation of the price of car per year?

A. 15%

B. 20%

C. 25%

D. 30%

38) A ladder leans against a wall forming a 60° angle between the ground and the ladder. If the bottom of the ladder is 30 feet away from the wall, how long is the ladder?

A. 30 $feet$

B. 40 $feet$

C. 50 $feet$

D. 60 $feet$

39) Anita's trick–or–treat bag contains 12 pieces of chocolate, 18 suckers, 18 pieces of gum, 24 pieces of licorice. If she randomly pulls a piece of candy from her bag, what is the probability of her pulling out a piece of sucker?

A. $\frac{1}{3}$

B. $\frac{1}{4}$

C. $\frac{1}{6}$

D. $\frac{1}{12}$

40) If $x + y = 0$, $4x - 2y = 24$, which of the following ordered pairs (x, y) satisfies both equations?

A. $(4, 3)$

B. $(5, 4)$

C. $(4, -4)$

D. $(4, -6)$

41) If $f(x) = 3x + 4(x + 1) + 2$ then $f(3x) = ?$

A. $21x + 6$

B. $16x - 6$

C. $25x + 4$

D. $12x + 3$

42) A line in the xy-plane passes through origin and has a slope of $\frac{2}{3}$. Which of the following points lies on the line?

A. $(2,1)$

B. $(4,1)$

C. $(9,6)$

D. $(9,3)$

43) Which of the following is equivalent to $(3n^2 + 4n + 6) - (2n^2 - 5)$?

A. $n + 4n^2$

B. $n^2 - 3$

C. $n^2 + 4n + 11$

D. $n + 2$

44) If $(ax + 4)(bx + 3) = 10x^2 + cx + 12$ for all values of x and $a + b = 7$, what are the two possible values for c?

A. $22, 21$

B. $20, 22$

C. $23, 26$

D. $24, 23$

45) Point A lies on the line with equation $y - 3 = 2(x + 5)$. If the x −coordinate of A is 8, what is the y −coordinate of A?

A. 14

B. 16

C. 22

D. 29

$$y < a - x \, , \, y > x + b$$

46) In the xy-plane, if $(0, 0)$ is a solution to the system of inequalities above, which of the following relationships between a and b must be true?

A. $a < b$

B. $a > b$

C. $a = b$

D. $a = b + a$

47) Which of the following points lies on the line that goes through the points $(2, 4)$ and $(4, 5)$?

A. $(9, 9)$

B. $(9, 6)$

C. $(6, 9)$

D. $(6, 6)$

48) Calculate $f(4)$ for the following function f.

$$f(x) = x^2 - 3x$$

A. 0

B. 4

C. 12

D. 20

49) John buys a pepper plant that is 6 inches tall. With regular watering the plant grows 4 inches a year. Writing John's plant's height as a function of time, what does the $y-$intercept represent?

A. The $y-$intercept represents the rate of grows of the plant which is 4 inches

B. The $y-$intercept represents the starting height of 6 inches

C. The $y-$intercept represents the rate of growth of plant which is 4 inches per year

D. There is no $y-$intercept

50) If $\frac{3}{x} = \frac{12}{x-9}$ what is the value of $\frac{x}{6}$?

A. -2

B. 2

C. $-\frac{1}{2}$

D. $\frac{1}{2}$

End of Math Practice Test 2.

Math Practice Tests Answer Keys

Now, it's time to review your results to see where you went wrong and what areas you need to improve.

Math Practice Test 1						Math Practice Test 2					
1	C	21	D	41	D	1	C	21	C	41	A
2	D	22	D	42	C	2	B	22	C	42	C
3	D	23	B	43	B	3	C	23	B	43	C
4	D	24	A	44	D	4	B	24	C	44	C
5	B	25	D	45	C	5	A	25	D	45	D
6	C	26	A	46	D	6	C	26	D	46	B
7	D	27	D	47	A	7	D	27	C	47	D
8	C	28	B	48	D	8	D	28	C	48	B
9	B	29	C	49	A	9	C	29	D	49	B
10	D	30	D	50	D	10	D	30	D	50	C
11	B	31	C			11	C	31	D		
12	D	32	C			12	B	32	D		
13	C	33	D			13	B	33	D		
14	D	34	D			14	A	34	D		
15	B	35	D			15	C	35	C		
16	B	36	B			16	B	36	B		
17	D	37	D			17	B	37	B		
18	A	38	D			18	B	38	D		
19	C	39	C			19	B	39	B		
20	D	40	A			20	C	40	C		

Math Practice Tests Answers and Explanations

Math Practice Test 1
Answers and Explanations

1) Choice C is correct

$$average\ (mean) = \frac{\text{sum of terms}}{\text{number of terms}} \Rightarrow 90 = \frac{sum\ of\ terms}{50} \Rightarrow sum = 90 \times 50 = 4500$$

The difference of 94 and 69 is 25. Therefore, 25 should be subtracted from the sum.

$$4500 - 25 = 4475,\ mean = \frac{\text{sum of terms}}{\text{number of terms}} \Rightarrow mean = \frac{4475}{50} = 89.5$$

2) Choice D is correct

For sum of 5: (1 & 4) *and* (4 & 1), (2 & 3) and (3 & 2), therefore we have 4 options.

For sum of 8: (5 & 3) *and* (3 & 5), (4 & 4) and (2 & 6), and (6 & 2), we have 5 options. To get a sum of 5 or 8 for two dice: $4 + 5 = 9$. Since, we have $6 \times 6 = 36$ total number of options, the probability of getting a sum of 5 and 8 is 9 out of 36 or $\frac{9}{36} = \frac{1}{4}$

3) Choice D is correct

Use FOIL method. $(5x + 2y)(2x - y) = 10x^2 - 5xy + 4xy - 2y^2 = 10x^2 - xy - 2y^2$

4) Choice D is correct

To solve absolute values equations, write two equations. $x - 10$ could be positive 4, or negative 4. Therefore, $x - 10 = 4 \Rightarrow x = 14$, $x - 10 = -4 \Rightarrow x = 6$. Find the product of solutions: $6 \times 14 = 84$

5) Choice B is correct

The equation of a line in slope intercept form is: $y = mx + b$. Solve for y.

$4x - 2y = 6 \Rightarrow -2y = 6 - 4x \Rightarrow y = (6 - 4x) \div (-2) \Rightarrow y = 2x - 3$. The slope is 2.

The slope of the line perpendicular to this line is: $m_1 \times m_2 = -1 \Rightarrow 2 \times m_2 = -1 \Rightarrow m_2 = -\frac{1}{2}$.

6) Choice C is correct

Plug in the value of x and y. $x = 3$ and $y = -2$.

$6(x - 2y) + (2 - x)^2 = 6(3 - 2(-2)) + (2 - 3)^2 = 6(3 + 4) + (-1)^2 = 42 + 1 = 43$

7) Choice D is correct

Use formula of rectangle prism volume. $V = (length)\,(width)\,(height) \Rightarrow 2500 = (25)\,(10)\,(height) \Rightarrow height = 2500 \div 250 = 10$

8) Choice C is correct

$4 \div \frac{1}{3} = 12$

9) Choice B is correct

The diagonal of the square is 4. Let x be the side. Use Pythagorean Theorem: $a^2 + b^2 = c^2$

$x^2 + x^2 = 4^2 \Rightarrow 2x^2 = 4^2 \Rightarrow 2x^2 = 16 \Rightarrow x^2 = 8 \Rightarrow x = \sqrt{8}$

The area of the square is: $\sqrt{8} \times \sqrt{8} = 8$

10) Choice D is correct

Solve for the sum of five numbers.

$\text{average} = \frac{\text{sum of terms}}{\text{number of terms}} \Rightarrow 26 = \frac{\text{sum of 5 numbers}}{5} \Rightarrow \text{sum of } 5 \text{ numbers} = 26 \times 5 = 130$

The sum of 5 numbers is 130. If a sixth number 42 is added, then the sum of 6 numbers is

$130 + 42 = 172.\ \text{average} = \frac{\text{sum of terms}}{\text{number of terms}} = \frac{172}{6} = 28.66$

11) Choice B is correct

ratio of A: $\frac{570}{600} = 0.95$; ratio of B: $\frac{291}{300} = 0.97$; ratio of C: $\frac{665}{700} = 0.95$ ratio   of   D:

$\frac{528}{550} = 0.96$

The maximum ratio is 0.97.

12) Choice D is correct

First find percentage of men in city A and percentage of women in city C.

Percentage of men in city A $= \frac{600}{1170}$ and percentage of women in city C $= \frac{665}{1365}$. Find

the ratio and simplify. $\frac{\frac{600}{1170}}{\frac{665}{1365}} = \frac{20}{19}$

13) Choice C is correct

$\frac{528 + x}{550} = 1.2 \rightarrow 528 + x = 660 \rightarrow x = 132$

14) Choice D is correct

Jason needs an 70% average to pass for five exams. Therefore, the sum of 5 exams must be at lease $5 \times 70 = 350$. The sum of 4 exams is: $68 + 72 + 85 + 90 = 315$.

The minimum score Jason can earn on his fifth and final test to pass is: $350 - 315 = 35$

15) Choice B is correct

Isolate and solve for $x. \frac{2}{3}x + \frac{1}{6} = \frac{1}{2} \Rightarrow \frac{2}{3}x = \frac{1}{2} - \frac{1}{6} = \frac{1}{3} \Rightarrow \frac{2}{3}x = \frac{1}{3}$. Multiply both sides

by the reciprocal of the coefficient of $x. \left(\frac{3}{2}\right)\frac{2}{3}x = \frac{1}{3}\left(\frac{3}{2}\right) \Rightarrow x = \frac{3}{6} = \frac{1}{2}$

16) Choice B is correct

Use simple interest formula: $I = prt$ ($I =$ interest, $p =$ principal, $r =$ rate, $t =$ time).

$I = (12,000)(0.045)(2) = 1,080$

17) Choice D is correct

Simplify. $7x^2y^3(2x^2y)^3 = 7x^2y^3(8x^6y^3) = 56x^8y^6$

18) Choice A is correct

Surface Area of a cylinder $= 2\pi r (r + h)$, The radius of the cylinder is 2 $(4 \div 2)$ inches and its height is 8 inches. Therefore, Surface Area of a cylinder $= 2\pi (2) (2 + 8) = 40\pi$

19) Choice C is correct

Three times of 25,000 is 75,000. One sixth of them cancelled their tickets. One sixth of 75,000 equals 12,500 $(\frac{1}{6} \times 75000 = 12500)$. 62,500 $(75000 - 12000 = 62500)$ fans are attending this week.

20) Choice D is correct

The area of the square is 49 inches. Therefore, the side of the square is square root of the area.

$\sqrt{49} = 7$ inches. Four times the side of the square is the perimeter: $4 \times 7 = 28\ inches$

21) Choice D is correct

$g(x) = -4$, then $f\big(g(x)\big) = f(-4) = 2(-4)^3 + 5(-4)^2 + 2(-4) = -128 + 80 - 8 = -56$

22) Choice D is correct

Use the information provided in the question to draw the shape.

Use Pythagorean Theorem: $a^2 + b^2 = c^2$

$50^2 + 120^2 = c^2 \Rightarrow 2,500 + 14,400 = c^2 \Rightarrow 16,900 = c^2 \Rightarrow$

$c = 130$

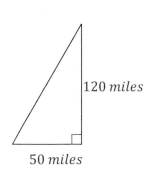

120 *miles*

Port A

50 *miles*

23) Choice B is correct

Plug in 104 for F and then solve for C.

$$C = \frac{5}{9}(F - 32) \Rightarrow C = \frac{5}{9}(104 - 32) \Rightarrow C = \frac{5}{9}(72) = 40$$

24) Choice A is correct

The width of the rectangle is twice its length. Let x be the length. Then, $width = 2x$

Perimeter of the rectangle is $2\,(width + length) = 2(2x + x) = 72 \Rightarrow 6x = 72 \Rightarrow x = 12$. Length of the rectangle is 12 meters.

25) Choice D is correct

$average = \frac{sum\ of\ terms}{number\ of\ terms} \Rightarrow$ (average of 6 numbers) $14 = \frac{sum\ of\ numbers}{6} \Rightarrow$ sum of 6 numbers is $14 \times 6 = 84$, (average of 4 numbers) $10 = \frac{sum\ of\ numbers}{4} \Rightarrow$ sum of 4 numbers is $10 \times 4 = 40$. $sum\ of\ 6\ numbers - sum\ of\ 4\ numbers = sum\ of\ 2\ numbers$,

$84 - 40 = 44$; average of 2 numbers $= \frac{44}{2} = 22$

26) Choice A is correct

First, find the number. Let x be the number. Write the equation and solve for x. 150% of a number is 75, then: $1.5 \times x = 75 \Rightarrow x = 75 \div 1.5 = 50$, 80% of 50 is: $0.8 \times 50 = 40$

27) Choice D is correct

Solve for y. $4x - 2y = 12 \Rightarrow -2y = 12 - 4x \Rightarrow y = 2x - 6$. The slope of the line is 2.

28) Choice B is correct

the population is increased by 10% and 20%. 10% increase changes the population to 110% of original population. For the second increase, multiply the result by 120%.

$(1.10) \times (1.20) = 1.32 = 132\%$. 32 percent of the population is increased after two years.

29) Choice C is correct

The formula for the area of the circle is: $A = \pi r^2$,The area is 36π. Therefore:$A = \pi r^2 \Rightarrow 6\pi = \pi r^2$, Divide both sides by π: $36 = r^2 \Rightarrow r = 6$. Diameter of a circle is $2 \times$ radius. Then:

$Diameter = 2 \times 6 = 12$

30) Choice D is correct

If 20% of a number is 4, what is the number: $20\% \ of \ x = 4 \Rightarrow 0.20 \ x = 4 \Rightarrow x = 4 \div 0.20 = 20$

31) Choice C is correct

Write a proportion and solve for x. $\frac{3}{2} = \frac{x}{26} \Rightarrow 2x = 3 \times 26 \Rightarrow x = 39 \ ft$

32) Choice C is correct

The distance between Jason and Joe is $9 \ miles$. Jason running at $6.5 \ miles \ per \ hour$ and Joe is running at the speed of $8 \ miles \ per \ hour$. Therefore, every hour the distance is $1.5 \ miles$ less.

$9 \div 1.5 = 6$

33) Choice D is correct

The failing rate is 11 out of 44 = $\frac{11}{44}$, Change the fraction to percent: $\frac{11}{44} \times 100\% =$ 25%. 25 percent of students failed. Therefore, 75 percent of students passed the exam.

34) Choice D is correct

$g(x) = -3,$ then $f(g(x)) = f(-3) = 2(-3)^3 + 5(-3)^2 + 2(-3) = -54 + 45 - 6 = -15$

35) Choice D is correct

Let x be the width of the rectangle. Use Pythagorean Theorem:

$a^2 + b^2 = c^2$

$x^2 + 6^2 = 10^2 \Rightarrow x^2 + 36 = 100 \Rightarrow x^2 = 100 - 36 = 64 \Rightarrow x = 8$

Perimeter of the rectangle $= 2\,(length + width) = 2\,(8 + 6) = 2\,(14) = 28$

36) Choice B is correct

The perimeter of the trapezoid is 38 cm. Therefore, the missing side is:

$38 - 13 - 9 - 4 = 12$. Area of a trapezoid: $A = \frac{1}{2}h(b_1 + b_2) = \frac{1}{2}(12)(4 + 9) = 78$

37) Choice D is correct

$f(g(x)) = 2 \times (\frac{1}{x})^3 + 2 = \frac{2}{x^3} + 2$

38) Choice D is correct

Use the information provided in the question to draw the shape.

Use Pythagorean Theorem: $a^2 + b^2 = c^2$

$80^2 + 150^2 = c^2 \Rightarrow 6400 + 22500 = c^2 \Rightarrow 28900 = c^2 \Rightarrow c = 170$

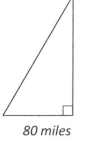

Port A

150 miles

80 miles

39) Choice C is correct

Write the ratio of $5a$ to $2b$. $\frac{5a}{2b} = \frac{1}{10}$. Use cross multiplication and then simplify.

$$5a \times 10 = 2b \times 1 \rightarrow 50a = 2b \rightarrow a = \frac{2b}{50} = \frac{b}{25}$$

Now, find the ratio of a to b. $\frac{a}{b} = \frac{\frac{b}{25}}{b} \rightarrow \frac{b}{25} \div b = \frac{b}{25} \times \frac{1}{b} = \frac{b}{25b} = \frac{1}{25}$

40) Choice A is correct

Plug in the value of x in the equation and solve for y. $2y = \frac{2x^2}{3} + 6 \rightarrow 2y = \frac{2(9)^2}{3} + 6 \rightarrow$

$$2y = \frac{2(81)}{3} + 6 \rightarrow 2y = 54 + 6 = 60 \rightarrow 2y = 60 \rightarrow y = 30$$

41) Choice D is correct

Since $N = 6$, substitute 6 for N in the equation $\frac{x-3}{5} = N$, which gives $\frac{x-3}{5} = 6$. Multiplying both sides of $\frac{x-3}{5} = 6$ by 5 gives $x - 3 = 30$ and then adding 3 to both sides of $x - 3 = 30$ then,

$x = 33$.

42) Choice C is correct

$b^{\frac{m}{n}} = \sqrt[n]{b^m}$ For any positive integers m and n. Thus, $b^{\frac{3}{5}} = \sqrt[5]{b^3}$

43) Choice B is correct

The total number of pages read by Sara is 3 (hours she spent reading) multiplied by her rate of reading: $\frac{N pages}{hour} \times 3 hours = 3N$

Similarly, the total number of pages read by Mary is 4 (hours she spent reading) multiplied by her rate of reading: $\frac{M pages}{hour} \times 4 hours = 4M$ the total number of pages read by Sara and Mary is the sum of the total number of pages read by Sara and the total number of pages read by Mary: $3N + 4M$.

44) Choice D is correct

The initial deposit earns 2 percent interest compounded annually. Thus, at the end of year 1, the new value of the account is the initial deposit of $150 plus 2 percent of the initial deposit:

$150 + \frac{2}{100}($150) = $150(1.02)$.

Since the interest is compounded annually, the value at the end of each succeeding year is the sum of the previous year's value plus 2 percent of the previous year's value. This is equivalent to multiplying the previous year's value by 1.02. Thus, after 2 years, the value will be $150(1.02)\ (1.02) = $(150)(1.02)^2$; and after 3 years, the value will be $(150)(1.02)^3$; and after n years, the value will be $(150)(1.02)^n$. Therefore, in the formula for the value for Sara's account after n years $(100)(x)^n$, the value of x is 1.02.

45) Choice C is correct

First find the value of b, and then find $f(5)$. Since $f(2) = 35$, substuting 2 for x and 35 for $f(x)$ gives $35 = b(2)^2 + 15 = 4b + 15$. Solving this equation gives $b = 5$. Thus

$$f(x) = 5x^2 + 15, \quad f(5) = 5(5)^2 + 15 \rightarrow f(5) = 125 + 15, \quad f(3) = 140$$

46) Choice D is correct

Solving Systems of Equations by Elimination: Multiply the first equation by (-2), then add it to the second equation.

$$\begin{array}{l} -2(2x + 5y = 11) \\ \underline{\quad 4x - 2y = -14 \quad} \end{array} \Rightarrow \begin{array}{l} -4x - 10y = -22 \\ \underline{\quad 4x - 2y = -14 \quad} \end{array} \Rightarrow -12y = -36 \Rightarrow y = 3$$

Plug in the value of y into one of the equations and solve for x.

$$2x + 5(3) = 11 \Rightarrow 2x + 15 = 11 \Rightarrow 2x = -4 \Rightarrow x = -2$$

47) Choice A is correct

Identify the input value. Since the function is in the form $f(x)$ and the question asks to calculate $f(4)$, the input value is four. $f(4) \rightarrow x = 4$, Using the function, input the desired x value. Now substitute 4 in for every x in the function. $f(x) = 3x^2 - 4$, $f(4) = 3(4)^2 - 4$, $f(4) = 48 - 4$, $f(4) = 44$

48) Choice D is correct

Frist factor the function: $f(x) = x^3 + 5x^2 + 6x = x(x+2)(x+3)$, To find the zeros, $f(x)$ should be zero. $f(x) = x(x+2)(x+3) = 0$, Therefore, the zeros are: $x = 0$, $(x+2) = 0 \Rightarrow x = -2$, $(x+3) = 0 \Rightarrow x = -3$

49) Choice A is correct

First write the equation in slope intercept form. Add $2x$ to both sides to get $6y = 2x + 24$. Now divide both sides by 6 to get $y = \frac{1}{3}x + 4$. The slope of this line is $\frac{1}{3}$, so any line that also has a slope of $\frac{1}{3}$ would be parallel to it. Only choice A has a slope of $\frac{1}{3}$.

50) Choice D is correct

$average = \frac{sum\ of\ terms}{number\ of\ terms} \Rightarrow 20 = \frac{13+15+20+x}{4} \Rightarrow 80 = 48 + x \Rightarrow x = 32$

Math Practice Test 2
Answers and Explanations

1) Choice C is correct

Let x be the number. Write the equation and solve for $x.(24 - x) \div x = 3$. Multiply both sides by x. $(24 - x) = 3x$, then add x both sides. $24 = 4x$, now divide both sides by 4.

$x = 6$

2) Choice B is correct

The sum of supplement angles is 180. Let x be that angle. Therefore, $x + 5x = 180$

$6x = 180$, divide both sides by 6: $x = 30$

3) Choice C is correct

The average speed of john is: $150 \div 6 = 25$, The average speed of Alice is: $180 \div 4 = 45$

Write the ratio and simplify. $25 : 45 \Rightarrow 5 : 9$

4) Choice B is correct

The percent of girls playing tennis is: $40\% \times 35\% = 0.40 \times 0.35 = 0.14 = 14\%$

5) Choice A is correct

The sum of all angles in a quadrilateral is 360 degrees. Let x be the smallest angle in the quadrilateral. Then the angles are: $x, 2x, 3x, 4x,$

$x + 2x + 3x + 4x = 360 \rightarrow 10x = 360 \rightarrow x = 36$, The angles in the quadrilateral are: $36°, 72°, 108°,$ and $144°$, The smallest angle is 36 degrees.

6) Choice C is correct

Use distance formula: $Distance = Rate \times time \Rightarrow 420 = 50 \times T$, divide both sides by 50. $420 \div 50 = T \Rightarrow T = 8.4\ hours$. Change hours to minutes for the decimal part. $0.4\ hours = 0.4 \times 60 = 24\ minutes$.

7) Choice D is correct

Use Pythagorean Theorem: $a^2 + b^2 = c^2$, $6^2 + 8^{\ 2} = c^2 \Rightarrow 100 = c^2 \Rightarrow c = 10$

8) Choice D is correct

The ratio of boy to girls is $2:3$. Therefore, there are 2 boys out of 5 students. To find the answer, first divide the total number of students by 5, then multiply the result by 2.

$600 \div 5 = 120 \Rightarrow 120 \times 2 = 240$

9) Choice C is correct

Use percent formula: $part = \dfrac{percent}{100} \times whole$

$25 = \dfrac{percent}{100} \times 20 \Rightarrow 25 = \dfrac{percent \times 20}{100} \Rightarrow 25 = \dfrac{percent \times 2}{10}$, $multiply\ both\ sides\ by\ 10.$

$250 = percent \times 2$, divide both sides by 2. $125 = percent$

10) Choice D is correct

The perimeter of the trapezoid is 56.
Therefore, the missing side is $= 56 - 17 - 16 - 8 = 15$
Area of a trapezoid: $A = \dfrac{1}{2}h(b_1 + b_2) = \dfrac{1}{2}(15)(8 + 16) = \dfrac{1}{2}(15)(24) = 180$

11) Choice C is correct

Let x be the number. Write the equation and solve for x. $\dfrac{2}{3} \times 18 = \dfrac{2}{5} \cdot x \Rightarrow \dfrac{2 \times 18}{3} = \dfrac{2x}{5}$, use cross multiplication to solve for x. $5 \times 36 = 2x \times 3 \Rightarrow 180 = 6x \Rightarrow x = 30$

12) Choice B is correct

To find the discount, multiply the number by $(100\% - rate\ of\ discount)$.

Therefore, for the first discount we get: $(D)\ (100\% - 20\%) = (D)\ (0.80) = 0.80\ D$

For increase of 10%: $(0.80\ D)(100\% + 10\%) = (0.80\ D)(1.10) = 0.88\ D = 88\%\ of\ D$

13) Choice B is correct

Use the formula of areas of circles. $Area = \pi r^2 \Rightarrow 25\ \pi = \pi r^2 \Rightarrow 25 = r^2 \Rightarrow r = 5$

Radius of the circle is 5. Now, use the circumference formula: $Circumference = 2\pi r = 2\pi\ (5) = 10\ \pi$

14) Choice A is correct

Let x be the number of years. Therefore, $3,000 per year equals 2,000x. starting from $24,000 annual salary means you should add that amount to 3,000x. Income more than that is:

$I > 3,000\ x + 24,000$

15) Choice C is correct

The question is this: 1.75 is what percent of 1.25? Use percent formula: $part = \frac{percent}{100} \times whole$

$1.75 = \frac{percent}{100} \times 1.25 \Rightarrow 1.75 = \frac{percent \times 1.25}{100} \Rightarrow 175 = percent \times 1.25 \Rightarrow percent = \frac{175}{1.25} = 140$

16) Choice B is correct

Use the information provided in the question to draw the shape.

Use Pythagorean Theorem: $a^2 + b^2 = c^2$

$40^2 + 30^2 = c^2 \Rightarrow 1600 + 900 = c^2 \Rightarrow 2500 = c^2 \Rightarrow c = 50$

17) Choice B is correct

The question is this: 530.40 is what percent of 624?

Use percent formula: part $= \dfrac{\text{percent}}{100} \times$ whole. $530.40 = \dfrac{percent}{100} \times 624 \Rightarrow$

$530.40 = \dfrac{percent \times 624}{100} \Rightarrow 53040 = percent \times 624 \Rightarrow percent = \dfrac{530.40}{624} = 85$

530.40 is 85% of 624. Therefore, the discount is: $100\% - 85\% = 15\%$

18) Choice B is correct

If the score of Mia was 60, therefore the score of Ava is 30. Since, the score of Emma was half as that of Ava, therefore, the score of Emma is 15.

19) Choice B is correct

Let x be the smallest number. Then, these are the numbers: $x, x + 1, x + 2, x + 3, x + 4$

$average = \dfrac{\text{sum of terms}}{\text{number of terms}} \Rightarrow 38 = \dfrac{x+(x+1)+(x+2)+(x+3)+(x+4)}{5} \Rightarrow 38 = \dfrac{5x+10}{5} \Rightarrow 190 = 5x + 10 \Rightarrow 180 = 5x \Rightarrow x = 36$

20) Choice C is correct

The area of the floor is: $6 \, cm \times 24 \, cm = 144 \, cm^2$, The number is tiles needed $= 144 \div 8 = 18$

21) Choice C is correct

The weight of 12.2 meters of this rope is: $12.2 \times 600 \, g = 7320 \, g$,

$1 \, kg = 1000 \, g$, therefore, $7320 \, g \div 1000 = 7.32 \, kg$

22) Choice C is correct

4% of the volume of the solution is alcohol. Let x be the volume of the solution.

Then: $4\% \, of \, x = 24 \, ml \Rightarrow 0.04 \, x = 24 \Rightarrow x = 24 \div 0.04 = 600$

23) Choice B is correct

$average = \frac{sum \, of \, terms}{number \, of \, terms}$, The sum of the weight of all girls is: $18 \times 60 = 1080 \, kg$,

The sum of the weight of all boys is: $32 \times 62 = 1984 \, kg$, The sum of the weight

of all students is: $1080 + 1984 = 3064 \, kg$, average $= \frac{3064}{50} = 61.28$

24) Choice C is correct

Let x be the original price. If the price of a laptop is decreased by 10% to \$360,

then: $90\% \, of \, x = 360 \Rightarrow 0.90x = 360 \Rightarrow x = 360 \div 0.90 = 400$

25) Choice D is correct

Surface Area of a cylinder $= 2\pi r \, (r + h)$, The radius of the cylinder is 8 inches

and its height is 12 inches. Surface Area of a cylinder $= 2 \, (\pi) \, (8) \, (8 + 12) = 320 \, \pi$

26) Choice D is correct

$average = \frac{sum \, of \, terms}{number \, of \, terms} \Rightarrow 18 = \frac{13+15+20+x}{4} \Rightarrow 72 = 48 + x \Rightarrow x = 24$

27) Choice C is correct

Let x be the original price. If the price of the sofa is decreased by 25% to \$420,

then: $75\% \, of \, x = 420 \Rightarrow 0.75x = 420 \Rightarrow x = 420 \div 0.75 = 560$

28) Choice C is correct

Use simple interest formula:$I = prt$,(I = interest, p = principal, r = rate, t = time)

$I = (8,000)(0.045)(5) = 1,800$

29) Choice D is correct

$(4.2 \times 10^6) \times (2.6 \times 10^{-5}) = (4.2 \times 2.6) \times (10^6 \times 10^{-5}) = 10.92 \times (10^{6 + (-5)}) = 1.092 \times 10^2$

30) Choice D is correct

The formula of the volume of pyramid is: $V = \frac{l \times w \times h}{3}$. The length and width of the pyramid is $6\ cm$ and its height is $12\ cm$. Therefore:$V = \frac{6 \times 6 \times 12}{3} = 144\ cm^3$

31) Choice D is correct

Simplify:$4(x + 1) = 6(x - 4) + 20, 4x + 4 = 6x - 24 + 20, 4x + 4 = 6x - 4$

Subtract $4x$ from both sides:$4 = 2x - 4$,Add 4 to both sides:$8 = 2x, 4 = x$

32) Choice D is correct

Use distributive property: $2x(4 + 2y) = 8x + 4xy = 4xy + 8x$

33) Choice D is correct

$y = 4ab + 3b^3$, plug in the values of a and b in the equation: $a = 2$ and $b = 3$,

$y = 4ab + 3b^3 \rightarrow y = 4(2)(3) + 3(3^3) = 24 + 81 = 105$

34) Choice D is correct

Solve for x. $-2 \leq 2x - 4 < 8 \Rightarrow$ (add 4 all sides) $-2 + 4 \leq 2x - 4 + 4 < 8 + 4 \Rightarrow$

$2 \leq 2x < 12 \Rightarrow$ (divide all sides by 2) $1 \leq x < 6$

x is between 1 and 6. Choice D represent this inequality.

35) Choice C is correct

Set of number that are not composite between 1 and 25: A= {1, 2, 3, 5, 7, 11, 13, 17, 19, 23}

$$\text{Probability} = \frac{number\ of\ desired\ outcomes}{number\ of\ total\ outcomes} = \frac{10}{25} = \frac{2}{5}$$

36) Choice B is correct

Plug in each pair of number in the equation:

A. $(2, 1)$: $2\,(2) + 4\,(1) = 8$

B. $(-1, 3)$: $2\,(-1) + 4\,(3) = 10$

C. $(-2, 2)$: $2\,(-2) + 4\,(2) = 4$

D. $(2, 2)$: $2\,(2) + 4\,(2) = 12$

Only Choice B is correct.

37) Choice B is correct

Use this formula: Percent of Change: $\frac{\text{New Value} - \text{Old Value}}{\text{Old Value}} \times 100\%$

$$\frac{16000 - 20000}{20000} \times 100\% = -20\% \text{ and } \frac{12800 - 16000}{16000} \times 100\% = -20\%$$

38) Choice D is correct

The relationship among all sides of special right triangle

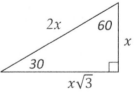

$30° - 60° - 90°$ is provided in this triangle:

In this triangle, the opposite side of $30°$ angle is half of the hypotenuse.

Draw the shape of this question:

The ladder is the hypotenuse. Therefore, the ladder is $60\ ft$

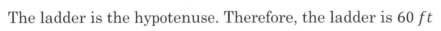

39) Choice B is correct

$$\text{Probability} = \frac{number\ of\ desired\ outcomes}{number\ of\ total\ outcomes} = \frac{18}{12+18+18+24} = \frac{18}{72} = \frac{1}{4}$$

40) Choice C is correct

Method 1: Plugin the values of x and y provided in the options into both equations.

A. $(4, 3)$ $x + y = 0 \rightarrow 4 + 3 \neq 0$

B. $(5, 4)$ $x + y = 0 \rightarrow 5 + 4 \neq 0$

C. $(4, -4)$ $x + y = 0 \rightarrow 4 + (-4) = 0$

D. $(4, -6)$ $x + y = 0 \rightarrow 4 + (-6) \neq 0$

Only option C is correct.

Method 2: Multiplying each side of $x + y = 0$ by 2 gives $2x + 2y = 0$. Then, adding the corresponding side of $2x + 2y = 0$ and $4x - 2y = 24$ gives $6x = 24$. Dividing each side of $6x = 24$ by 6 gives $x = 4$. Finally, substituting 4 for x in $x + y = 0$, or $y = -4$. Therefore, the solution to the given system of equations is $(4, -4)$.

41) Choice A is correct

If $f(x) = 3x + 4(x + 1) + 2$, then find $f(3x)$ by substituting $3x$ for every x in the function. This gives: $f(3x) = 3(3x) + 4(3x + 1) + 2$

It simplifies to: $f(3x) = 3(3x) + 4(3x + 1) + 2 = 9x + 12x + 4 + 2 = 21x + 6$

42) Choice C is correct

First, find the equation of the line. All lines through the origin are of the form $y = mx$, so the equation is $y = \frac{2}{3}x$. Of the given choices, only choice C (9,6), satisfies this equation:

$$y = \frac{2}{3}x \rightarrow 6 = \frac{2}{3}(9) = 6$$

43) Choice C is correct

$(3n^2 + 4n + 6) - (2n^2 - 5)$. Add like terms together: $3n^2 - 2n^2 = n^2$

$4n$ doesn't have like terms. $6 - (-5) = 11$

Combine these terms into one expression to find the answer: $n^2 + 4n + 11$

44) Choice C is correct

You can find the possible values of a and b in $(ax + 4)(bx + 3)$ by using the given equation $a + b = 7$ and finding another equation that relates the variables a and b. Since $(ax + 4)(bx + 3) = 10x^2 + cx + 12$, expand the left side of the equation to obtain

$$abx^2 + 4bx + 3ax + 12 = 10x^2 + cx + 12$$

Since ab is the coefficient of x^2 on the left side of the equation and 10 is the coefficient of x^2 on the right side of the equation, it must be true that $ab = 10$

The coefficient of x on the left side is $4b + 3a$ and the coefficient of x in the right side is c. Then: $4b + 3a = c$, $\qquad\qquad$ $a + b = 7$, then: $a = 7 - b$

Now, plug in the value of a in the equation $ab = 10$. Then:

$$ab = 10 \rightarrow (7 - b)b = 10 \rightarrow 7b - b^2 = 10$$

Add $-7b + b^2$ both sides. Then: $b^2 - 7b + 10 = 0$

Solve for b using the factoring method. $b^2 - 7b + 10 = 0 \rightarrow (b - 5)(b - 2) = 0$

Thus, either $b = 2$ and $a = 5$, or $b = 5$ and $a = 2$. If $b = 2$ and $a = 5$, then

$4b + 3a = c \rightarrow 4(2) + 3(5) = c \rightarrow c = 23$. If $5 = 2$ and $a = 2$, then, $4b + 3a = c \rightarrow 4(5) + 3(2) = c \rightarrow c = 26$. Therefore, the two possible values for c are 23 and 26.

45) Choice D is correct

Here we can substitute 8 for x in the equation. Thus, $y - 3 = 2(8 + 5)$, $y - 3 = 26$

Adding 3 to both side of the equation: $y = 26 + 3$, $\qquad y = 29$

46) Choice B is correct

Since $(0, 0)$ is a solution to the system of inequalities, substituting 0 for x and 0 for y in the given system must result in two true inequalities. After this substitution, $y < a - x$ becomes $0 < a$, and $y > x + b$ becomes $0 > b$. Hence, a is positive and b is negative. Therefore, $a > b$.

47) Choice D is correct

First find the slope of the line using the slope formula. $m = \frac{y_2 - y_1}{x_2 - x_1}$

Substituting in the known information. $(x_1, y_1) = (2, 4)$, $\quad (x_2, y_2) = (4, 5)$

$m = \frac{5 - 4}{4 - 2} = \frac{1}{2}$

Now the slope to find the equation of the line passing through these points. $y = mx + b$

Choose one of the points and plug in the values of x and y in the equation to solve for b.

Let's choose point $(4, 5)$. Then: $y = mx + b \rightarrow 5 = \frac{1}{2}(4) + b \rightarrow 5 = 2 + b \rightarrow b = 5 - 2 = 3$

The equation of the line is: $y = \frac{1}{2}x + 3$

Now, plug in the points provided in the choices into the equation of the line.

A. $(9, 9)$ $\qquad y = \frac{1}{2}x + 3 \rightarrow 9 = \frac{1}{2}(9) + 3 \rightarrow 9 = 7.5$ $\qquad$ This is NOT true.

B. $(9, 6)$ $\qquad y = \frac{1}{2}x + 3 \rightarrow 6 = \frac{1}{2}(9) + 3 \rightarrow 6 = 7.5$ $\qquad$ This is NOT true.

C. $(6, 9)$ $\qquad y = \frac{1}{2}x + 3 \rightarrow 9 = \frac{1}{2}(6) + 3 \rightarrow 9 = 6$ $\qquad$ This is NOT true.

D. $(6, 6)$ $\qquad y = \frac{1}{2}x + 3 \rightarrow 6 = \frac{1}{2}(6) + 3 \rightarrow 6 = 6$ $\qquad$ This is true!

Therefore, the only point from the choices that lies on the line is $(6, 6)$.

48) Choice B is correct

The input value is 4. Then: $x = 4$

$$f(x) = x^2 - 3x \rightarrow f(4) = 4^2 - 3(4) = 16 - 12 = 4$$

49) Choice B is correct

To solve this problem, first recall the equation of a line: $y = mx + b$

Where $m = slope$. $y = y - intercept$

Remember that slope is the rate of change that occurs in a function and that the $y -$intercept is the y value corresponding to $x = 0$. Since the height of John's plant is 6 inches tall when he gets it. Time (or x) is zero. The plant grows 4 inches per year. Therefore, the rate of change of the plant's height is 4. The $y -$intercept represents the starting height of the plant which is 6 inches.

50) Choice C is correct

Multiplying each side of $\frac{3}{x} = \frac{12}{x-9}$ by $x(x - 9)$ gives $3(x - 9) = 12(x)$, distributing the 3 over the values within the parentheses yields $x - 9 = 4x$ or $x = -3$.

Therefore, the value of $\frac{x}{6} = \frac{-3}{6} = -\frac{1}{2}$.

Receive the PDF version of this book or get another FREE book!

Thank you for using our Book!

Do you LOVE this book?

Then, you can get the PDF version of this book or another book absolutely FREE!

Please email us at:

info@EffortlessMath.com

for details.

Author's Final Note

As you've turned the final page of "***Adult Math for Beginners***," I hope you feel a sense of pride in advancing your mathematical understanding. Well done!

Your choice of this guide from the myriad of options means a great deal to me, and I am grateful for your trust in enhancing your mathematical foundation. Your dedication to improving your skills is truly praiseworthy.

This book was crafted with devotion, drawing upon extensive experience in teaching adults and acknowledging the distinct challenges they face. It was my aim to simplify mathematical concepts, offering you a firm base to build upon, be it for personal enrichment, career advancement, or academic readiness.

For any queries or clarifications needed for the topics discussed, please feel free to contact me at reza@effortlessmath.com, where I'll be eager to provide assistance. Your feedback is also crucial for the refinement of this book. Any inconsistencies or suggestions for improvement you come across are welcomed; your insights lead the way for future editions.

If you've found value in this book, I'd be delighted to hear about your journey. Leaving a brief comment or review on Amazon would greatly support my work and also assist your peers in their mathematical pursuits. To leave your valuable feedback, please visit: bit.ly/3FQrZwy

Or scan this QR code.

Your feedback is earnestly considered, as it's my commitment to offer a resource that stands as a true ally for adults reengaging with math.

Thank you for your encouragement. I extend my best wishes for your continued mathematical success!

Reza Nazari

Math teacher and author

Printed in Great Britain
by Amazon

42992434R00110